Through Many Bridges

Celebrating the Seasons

by
Amelia W. Fletcher

FACTOR PRESS
P.O. Box 8888
Mobile, Alabama 36608

Second printing, January 1998

ISBN 1-887650-07-5

Cover painting by
Teresa Harris Mathews

Through Many Bridges
Celebrating the Seasons

WINTER

Predictions
Bowl Game Syndrome
Ritual
Cool Conversations
Beauty Shop Philosophy
Things That Go Bump
Rip-Off
First Word In Diet
Fat Tuesday
Valentine's Day
What We Do For Love
Map Reading
Cleaning Closets

SPRING

Slinky In My Dreams
How My Garden Grows
Address Book
Gone Buggy
D Day
My Dream House
Tee Off
Grazing
Hear Ye
Stuck Up!
Lights Out!
Battle Of The Sections
Wishing On A Star
Nightmare On Express Lane
Easter Hunt
Cold War
Procrastination Pros
Chocolate Covered Easter
A Type "A+" Mother

SUMMER

Ah! Vacation
Suiting Myself
Survival on Hwy 59
Stiff Stuff
There Are Some Days

Thunderstruck
Puzzle
Survival Of The Fittest
Necessities Of Packing
Just Waitin' For The Camera
Throwing In The Towel
Plumbing
ATM's
Catalog Queen

FALL

Labor Day
Sounds Of Fall
Getting The Blues
Buying School Supplies
List And Tales
A Biting Tale
Sacked
In The Sun
Weather Channel
No Deposit, No Return
Computer II
Approach To Cleaning
All The World's A Stage
Seasonal Searches
Gone Camping
Car Phone
Doing Time

HOLIDAYS

November Conversations
Veterans' Day
Veterans' Day Salute
Simple Thanks
Thanks A Lot
Stuffed Turkey
Open Letter
Christmas Shopping
On, Dasher
Oh, Christmas Tree
Christmas Lights
No-Bake Christmas
All Wrapped Up
First One Up
A Good Christmas Laugh
Ready And Set

Through Many Bridges

Foreword

We are a typical American family: working folks, children, pets. The daily routines of our lives connect one year to the next as we laugh, struggle, work, and play. As we build bridges to friends and family, we also cross bridges of challenge, and amble through many bridges splendidly decorated with the seasons. Perhaps in the true philosophy of the Romantics, our family experiences much to reflect upon later.

The passage of time puts so many bridges into focus: My parents have instilled my basic values with lots of love; my brothers and their families have proven over and over again the "family first" philosophy works; and aunts, uncles, and dear friends have sheltered me like the branches of a huge water oak. Yet, it is with a smile and a prayer that I want to say a big thank you to my children, who have eaten lots of frozen dinners and done their own laundry in order for me to type, and to Ken, the Hon who is always in my corner and by my side.

To my Great Aunt Gay, my longtime and faithful mentor, I want to say a special thanks. She fanned and nurtured the creative spark she saw in a shy little girl long ago.

As the seasons flow from one into another, I have developed a sober respect for every episode and every individual in my life. Each makes the reflection of the bridges of my lifetime continuously beautiful.

Winter Bridges

The short, cold days of January settle in and cover us with its gray blanket. Yet, by the crackling log fire and the warmth of loved ones close, winter offers the celebration of life: the brisk excitement of New Year's Day ball games, the fluttering of emotions on Valentine's Day, the carnival air of Mardi Gras. M-mmmm...winter bridges are never dull.

Predictions

There are a few things in life that are givens, as the old adage goes: death and taxes. Everything else is fair game for prognosticators. I glance at their predictions every year when flipping through the January magazines and get a good chuckle. The grand dames of the mystic world tell awaiting crowds who will marry, who will divorce; who will be successful, who will fail.

This year I thought I'd give it a whirl. So, instead of my straw Panama, I donned a turban, found the biggest ring I own for my finger, and all the bracelets in the panhandle. Got my paperweight with the snow scene and sat down at the kitchen table. Hey, I've seen enough movies to know how it's done and, remarkably, the spirits gave me the predictions.

Prediction #1: 95 percent of Americans will vow to lose weight, and .001 percent will actually manage to lose it and keep it off. The rest of us will lose 5 pounds, then gain 15.

Prediction #2: The fashion makers' attempts to return us to the clothes of the '70's will meet with only moderate success. The generations who have never worn bell-bottoms and mini-skirts will give them a whirl, the rest of us will just shake our heads and have nightmares about the dryer that shrank all those polyester pants and tops two sizes.

Prediction #3: Talk shows won't get any worse, but they won't get any better. Oprah will stay Queen of the Day, and Ricki will stay Queen of Sludge, and Jenny will want to just stay out of court.

Prediction #4: New computers and software will continue to give most of us a rash from frustration and produce a feeling of being left behind in a pile of outdated disks and hard drives in this strange world of technology. My mother's 1959 refrigerator still hums along, but my new computer programs of '96 are already obsolete. They won't even be compatible with '97, much less whatever state of the arts Windows will bring on the screen. It is all a plot.

Prediction #5: The remote control will remain lost, and I will spend another year trying to program the VCR.

Prediction #6: The Republicans will dig at the Democrats (and vice versa) and keep the mud mill in high gear. The inauguration will be the lull before the storm.

Prediction #7: Sadly, the wars of hatred sparked by centuries of mistrust will continue despite valiant efforts to mediate and negotiate.

Prediction #8: Most of us will manage to live our quiet lifestyle day in and day out without much ado. The predictions and prophecies will make little difference to us. But...

Prediction #9: We all wish and hope for cures and peace and understanding and a little more love today than yesterday...not bad!

So, from Sister Sand and her Snowball...have a Happy New Year!

Bowl Game Syndrome

"Doctor, I don't know what is wrong with him. He sits in his chair and twitches his fingers. Once in awhile, he slurps down a can of soda or yells 'Facemask.'" I spoke as I continuously kept wringing my hands in motherly frustration.

"Relax. I don't think there's very much wrong with your son. Let me ask a few leading questions, and maybe we can clear all this up in a matter of moments."

Son sat quietly in the small, sterile office, appearing to be in a dormant state. He had not spoken coherently or eaten in his normal frenzy since a couple of nights before New Year's Day. A mom is apt to be concerned when all of the goodies baked for the holidays have not been consumed with regular teenage energy.

The doctor peered deep into Son's blue eyes and began the serious questioning. "What's the score?"

Son shook as if taken by a deep chill and mumbled, "Twenty-seven to zero, with six seconds to play."

"Hm..m..m. Do you know which channel the Sugar Bowl is on?"

Again Son trembled and nodded. He raised his hand in front of himself zombie-like and extended it forward as if to get a good aim with the remote control. He flicked his thumb a couple of times and then contentedly smiled.

"Did you line up all three TV sets in the living room?"

At that point I interjected, "We looked like the headquarters for ESPN. I don't think there was a game on the air waves that we didn't get."

"Sit down a second, I think I have a diagnosis. Your child has Bowl Game Syndrome. It usually strikes males between the ages of 12 and 99. The syndrome is not serious or permanent. In a few days he'll be his old self...maybe a little thinner due to the lack of regular and good eating and sleeping habits." He patted me on the shoulder in sympathy as Son sighed deeply and seemed to fall asleep as gently as a babe.

I felt relieved and enlightened. I'd lived with and witnessed family and friends who, through the years, had been mildly touched by this peculiar syndrome.

"I've been through a lot of bridges to the New Year, but never one quite like this. Thanks, Doc. Hope you have a great New Year. I'll take this lad home and give him some chicken soup. That seems to cure most anything."

About that time, Son jumped up out of his slumber and yelled, "Kill the ref!" Then slumped back into the chair.

"This bowl game syndrome better not last too long. His note for school will read: 'Please excuse Son for his absence. Although his body is present, his mind will be back after a short break for local station identification.'" I wilted with resignation.

The doctor patted me on the shoulder and said in his best bedside voice, "Have a good day. See you next bowl season."

Ritual

After eating my way through the entire holidays, I begin one of my annual rituals: The January Diet. Just as the migratory birds and beasts know when to move along, my body must have a sense of knowing when enough is enough.

If sincerity lost pounds, I would be the size of a number 3 pencil. However, that's not the case, and when I can no longer get into my basic navy pants...well, I think you get the picture.

I succumb to media advertising, along with purchasing every green veggie possible in a well-stocked grocery. Chocolate flavors with no calories, cookies with fiber, and jump ropes with super-grip handles are just a few of the items now in my possession.

"Mom, you'll never look like that model on the refrigerator no matter what kind of cookies you eat," Son announced as he stacked three peanut butter and jelly sandwiches on a plate for an afternoon snack (dinner was an hour away). Knowing that he had gotten my attention, he continued the commentary. "You'd need suction surgery to get thighs like that on legs like yours!" If I had had a knife, I might have had tongue soup for my supper.

"That's okay, smarty. Someday you'll look like that baseball player, Tommy Lasorda, and make commercials for diet aids, and then I'll laugh." Of course, body flab is science fiction to a 15-year-old.

Sis said very little as she sneaked into the kitchen to plunder the cabinets. "I hate it when you diet. You never buy real food. What is there for me to eat? Can we go get a burger or pizza somewhere? Did you know that

Mary's mom lost twenty-five pounds in two weeks by having her jaws wired together?"

From deep within the living room, someone's voice supplied, "Hey, that would be great. Mom couldn't tell me to clean my room or take out the trash. That would be super."

"Well, I don't have my jaws wired. Neither am I brain dead, yet. Clean the peanut butter off this counter and don't wish for anything above thirty-five calories for supper."

"Wish!" Son sulked. "If I were sixteen, I could do the drive-throughs myself for more food while I chopped the next meal."

Cool Conversations

I was down to my last plastic dish with a top: It was time. I opened the refrigerator door and gave a loud moan. There was not a corner—nay, not half an inch of space—to put another leftover dish covered with plastic wrap, or a ziplock bag of salad.

"Guess I'll have to clean out the remains from Labor Day, Christmas, New Year, and weekends of cooking for company."

"Sweetheart, are you talking to yourself again?" asked Hon, as he reached past me to grab the milk jug. "I worry about you when you get that determined look on your face and stare into the refrigerator with the fierceness of the wicked queen in *Snow White* as she glared into her magic mirror. Hey, these apples aren't poison are they?"

"No, you mean there are apples in there? Maybe they're left from the Halloween treats." Fumbling and fussing, I discovered it was impossible to move anything; therefore, it became apparent that major removal was imperative. I started with the milk, soft drinks, ketchup, and orange juice. "It's going to be a long day."

"Sweetheart, are you talking to yourself again?" asked Hon, as he reached for the mayo. "I worry about you spending your free time doing all these unpleasant chores."

I ignored the comment and plucked from the back of the shelves covered dishes filled with penicillin mold, new life forms of green, and concoctions so far beyond recognition that they didn't even have a horrible smell. "Good grief, I should win a prize for the oldest casserole in the state. If I keep it long enough, it might end up in the Smithsonian as a petrified memento of this century."

I zeroed in on the crisper drawers. I yanked them open, only to groan again. "These carrots won't even be good in the casserole I just stuffed down the garbage disposal."

"Sweetheart, are you talking to yourself again?" asked Hon, as he stepped in front of me to check the door for his brand of mustard and pickles. "The game is in the third quarter. I'll help you after it's over if you want me to." His monotone gave away his lack of sincerity, and I didn't respond.

I wiped and swiped at the goo in the crinkles of the shelves. The manufactures of refrigerators must have a contest to see how many ridges and rills can be put in one unit. Pride rose in my mother's heart at being able to see the setting of the temperature gauge all the way on the back wall. "No wonder my fresh veggies froze! This thing is set to put frost on the nose of any poor soul who opens the door."

My hefty trash bags could have been featured in a commercial demonstrating their strength as I proceeded to the shelves on the door. There were jalapeno peppers the age of Sis, a sauce for Chinese food that I used once (at least a year ago), and jelly jars with one spoonful of jelly hugging the bottom, not to mention the empty jars of favorite sandwich spreads. "Nobody in this house throws away a jar or bottle of anything when it's empty but me!"

"Sweetheart, are you talking to yourself again?" asked Hon, as he suddenly developed a gaze of amazement akin to horror. "Where's all the stuff in the refrigerator? We've been robbed during the night!"

"Were you looking for something in particular? The ham from Christmas..., the potatoes from the church dinner? Too late! I've emptied and cleaned the entire fridge." He turned to survey the counters and sink. An explosion of food, bowls, jars, and lids littered the entire area. The kitchen appeared to have been plundered and pillaged by a hoard of teenagers. "This bridge obviously has an extension to it. Part two will have to be printed in the tabloids with the title 'Woman Disappears After Attack From Alien Hiding In Stack of Dirty Dishes.'" My voice trailed off.

"Sweetheart, you talk to yourself too much. Maybe you should get some rest. By the way, where is the wheat bread with the moldy edge? I can't make another sandwich since you've cleaned and vacuumed the ice box. Guess I'll just have to starve as I watch the fourth quarter!"

I was beyond words.

Beauty Shop Philosophy

I've always known, but never quite put into actual words, the reasons my mother's generation felt the need for weekly hair appointments. Today, with modern cuts and casual lifestyles, many women don't frequent the beauty shop every week. Perhaps once or twice a month could keep us in control of the tresses, until the newest phase: the full service salon. Beauticians are wise, and know that women are drawn together by some unknown power. If not hair, then nails, or a massage! Give the customer what she needs.

After several "bad hair days," I resolved to break down and get a haircut and a perm last Thursday. The girls at each station greeted me like a long lost loved one. I spent the next couple of hours after a hectic workday in "the chair." I sat quietly for a few minutes, then the gal doing my hair began her work and her conversation. After defining "how much and how curly," she asked a leading and loaded question: "How's your kids?"

As if the rock had been struck by Moses, an outpouring of worries, pride, and ponderings gushed forth. She heard everything from apples to zippers as she scrubbed and rinsed and rolled. The tables did turn and she had the same opportunity. Her teenager had gotten a speeding ticket, didn't like spinach for supper, needed some extra tutoring in math. Then there were phrases about a new horse which were drowned out by machines and interspersed with, "Hold you head down...close your eyes... sit up straight while I trim."

Under the dryer, I could hear snatches of conversation from the constant flow of patrons: O.J. and the assorted circus surrounding the event (I would dare say these gals knew more about the murder scene and the state of Marcia Clark's marriage than about the national deficit and the emerging bunch of presidential candidates).

Pickle recipes, craft projects (finished, unfinished, lost), the church supper coming up in a few days, bathing suits—all had supplements of opinion attached as scissors snipped, dryers hummed, and heads nodded.

If the gal said "uh-huh" once in her perceptive tone, she said it 50 times during the couple of hours I observed. Her hands deftly and methodically did their job; her ears and heart did the rest.

She patted and sprayed as she finished my do, whirled me around, and presented me with a mirror. (Funny, I felt as if I had *already* been gazing into a mirror.)

What a wonder. Beauticians and barbers don't collect for the haircut; they charge for the chair. That miraculous spot to let down our hair, to tell jokes, to purge the soul of kids and jobs, to hear out loud what's been troubling us, to expose the dreams—all in sometimes less than an hour.

"There. When would you like to come back, sweety?" I peered over the counter. The large appointment book seemed to be full! "I can squeeze you in on Tuesday two weeks from now."

"Fine." I would be able to cross this bridge again, even if I had to cancel something else. There would be room again. I gave a peaceful nod, took a deep breath, and felt like a pampered woman. Why not? I had a soothing scalp massage, a personal pick-me-up, and an analysis all in one visit. What a bargain!

Things That Go Bump!

"She's done it again!" Sis announced with frustration.

"Yeah, every two or three weeks there must be a virus she gets that gives her a temperature and makes her move furniture instead of throwing up!" Son replied.

"Did I hear you guys discussing the new arrangement of the den? I thought since the weather had changed, we would enjoy the couch and TV in a different place."

"Mom, one of these days I'm going to kill myself when I turn the corner with a glass of milk and run slap dab into the recliner." I noticed Son's tone did not have a note of tolerance in it. So, I turned my attention to his sister.

"Don't you like the way I put the fern next to the rocker? There was this picture in the March issue of a magazine I thought sorta looked like our place, but the furniture sat at angles instead...." Both kids were shaking their heads with dismay and mumbling comments to each other under their breaths.

"Do us a favor—don't start reading *101 Ways to Give Your Family Bruises and Nightmares* until I move out of the house. Okay?"

Son was emphatic, but I must confess I filed the statement for future use. I'd say in five or six years I can use it as ammunition to literally move him out and, yes, rearranging the furniture could be the trick.

"I kinda liked the den the way it used to be, and the plant blocks the screen," said Sis. "I may need to get the scissors after it."

Son stomped around the room, then asked, "Where's the Nintendo? I know you've hidden it. Is it in the plant? You will have to confess sooner or later."

I looked at Sis with disdain. At least she could have supported me in my creative efforts to make our homeplace comparable somewhat to the picture I had shown her. But no sympathy was to be found.

"Did you hide the phone, too?" asked Sis. Sheer panic instantly set in and I had to assure her that I did not nor would not hide her umbilical cord to the outside world.

From all of this, I learned that children are not as adaptable as Dr. Spock's book says, and that I get no respect for my designing endeavors. Yet, the urge to move the couch will strike again (and it strikes at the least predictable times). Son and Sis will have to suffer the injuries of obstacles replaced. Maybe I'll get my friend and her needlepoint stitcher to do me the familiar prayer to hang in my den: "Protect us from ghosties and beasties and things that go bump in the night."

Rip Off

"Mom, your face is as red as a beet. You haven't been trying to do the Jane Fonda exercise tape again, have you?" Sis had a true stare of concern on her face as she poked her head into the laundry room door.

"No, but I wish I was the Terminator or some other super hero right this minute. I bought this fifty pound bucket of laundry detergent so that I would be able to wash clothes to my heart's content and not run out before the end of May. We have to be the cleanest...."

"Mom, you're rambling again."

"No, I'm not. Let me finish. Today is Thursday, right? The day I like to get as much done as I can before the weekend. But, in order to wash my six washers of clothes, I have to be able to open this big blue bucket of washing powders."

"So, what's the problem?"

"I've read the directions and looked at the pictures, and it said to 'pull the tab.' I've pulled and yanked and tugged. The top won't come off. Go get me a sharp knife."

"Hey, it's not that bad. What kind do you want?"

"I'm going to cut a hole in the top. I need to get my dirty clothes washed and I've cussed and discussed this all I'm going to. Go get me a sharp knife."

Moments pass like hours. I beat the lid. Of course, I can't do too much with it because the stuff weighs more than my purse.

"Where is a strong arm when you need it?" I drone. "What does it matter? If I asked Son to do it, he would ask me to hand him sixteen tools, and then stand over him to observe what a wonderful job he would be doing. I don't have time for that, only to have him called away by one of his friends or by hunger pangs. I'd end up doing it myself or hiring it done."

"Mom, here's the knife, but if you don't stop talking to yourself, I'm going to turn you in for evaluation at the mental health clinic."

I jab a hole in the red plastic top and wrench at the lid until it pops off into my angry hands. "There's got to be a better way to put a lid on a bucket of detergent. This bridge is avoidable... gonna write a letter to *Consumer Reports*, or Ralph Nader."

"Hey, Mom, are you talking to yourself?" Son stooped over and tickled me.

"Where is a strong arm when you need one? Never mind, I know. You were at the gym lifting weights." I push on the bucket to place it in the corner next to the washer.

"Your face sure is red. Did you do your annual hour of exercise to that tape you have? You know, I could've opened that lid for you if you had asked me to." Son sauntered away and headed for the refrigerator.

"That's okay, I needed it done today."

First Word In Diet

"I made a New Year's resolution to lose fifteen pounds before Easter. Here it is February and I've eaten enough carrots to make Bugs Bunny jealous, and used Cher's brand of artificial sweetener. And what happens? I gain four pounds and am faced with a holiday made of chocolate hearts and cupids! The first three letters in diet are D-I-E!" I sat expounding my problems over coffee with my neighbor, the ultimate optimist.

"Oh, your body has just got to get used to living on low-fat foods. Anyway, the new fashions are great for hiding a little extra weight."

"Yeah, and they're perfect for pregnant women, too. The only good thing about big tops is that they come in dark, conservative colors. Hand me some celery stalks and stop being so cheerful."

"Well, you're being too hard on yourself. Remember that plump women have been fashionable through many centuries."

"Dear friend, this is not the age of Rubens. Too bad though, I could have a career as a model. If I had lived during the Crusades, I wouldn't have survived long enough to get fat, or at least I'd have my salt intake limited. Pour me a glass of that fizzy water that sells for two dollars a bottle."

"So, what's your next option? Have your jaws wired?"

"No, the only thing I'm going to have wired is my house for earphones so my nerves won't be jangled when the kids are playing their music video station, and I've had six cups of leaded coffee and no sleep."

"Aw, get a couple of those cute exercise outfits and sweat off those extra pounds. I'll join you."

"Misery does love company, but you've lost your mind. Have you seen those thong things with wild prints? We'd look like two hot air balloons bobbing to music."

"Here, why don't you have some yogurt. It has bananas and strawberries in it. How about one of those exercise videos? You know, Jane Fonda's Brains of Steel."

"*Buns* of Steel, *Buns*. It just makes me sick to see all those beautiful people with their carved bodies and thick hair. And you read all their workout programs in the magazines."

"I read one of those articles just last week. It outlined four famous women's routines: weights six hours a week, ten hours on the exercise bike, twenty hours jogging, and five in the sauna. Get up at four, eat bean sprouts, do a treadmill while negotiating a new contract, have twins one day and a new movie the next. And they all have long nails!"

"Don't believe a word. Besides, Madonna and Janet Jackson have different body types than we do. We're more like Marilyn Monroe or Liz. Forget the greens, hand me a cookie. Promise me you won't give me a deli tray of fresh vegetables with nonfat dressing for Valentine's Day. Okay?"

"Promise. Here, take a scoop of ice cream."

"Thanks. This bridge between the holidays has all of a sudden gotten more enjoyable. Let's see, Easter has chocolate bunnies, sugared birds, and ham! There's no letting up. Might as well make mine two scoops!"

Fat Tuesday

Everybody I know is on a diet, counting fat grams, or sweating to the oldies. It suggests an entirely different meaning of the term, "Fat Tuesday." Daily, I sit across from a lady eating carrot sticks and bean sprouts at lunch while I swirl spaghetti or dunk donuts. Of course, she's about the size of the carrot and I'm as rolypoly as the donut—the hole is in my head. Yet, here in the Lenten days after the riotous celebrations, I've determined to get slight and slinky before I literally roll into another bathing suit season.

Wednesday, my grocery cart did not contain one Mardi Gras king cake. Instead, it sprouted broccoli, celery, bagels, and cauliflower. No chips, no dip, no sour cream. Thank goodness for all the astonishing no-fat products. But, not only do they slim the waist, they also slim the pocketbook. I rolled home with bulging bags of no-fat goodies.

Hon was not impressed. The man has never read a nutrition label, has scoffed at chocolate cookies with no fat, and tossed aside the salad dressing with low calorie slogans. The only item to catch any special attention was the box of Special K. Hon gazed at me, then at the gal on the box, then shook his head. Not even in my dreams would I look like that in a white swimsuit. This leggy beauty was so tall, I wouldn't come to her waist even if I wore heels.

I tacked a "before and after" picture from one of those weight loss program ads at eye level on the refrigerator. Son got into the act and placed a picture of a 300-pound woman from the cover of a tabloid, with my face pasted on top, beside it. He had also taken a marker and written my initial across the skirt. I cried. He crossed out my initials and scribbled a mask on the face. It didn't help. Son soon discovered the meaning of fasting on bread and water.

No good weight loss program is complete without an exercise program. I set my alarm for 5:30 a.m. It went off as scheduled at 5:30. Three snooze buttons later, I was jumping out of bed. This turned out to be the only exercise I managed to get.

Folks, it's still dark at 5:30 a.m. So, I decided to experiment with exercise at 5:30 p.m. That didn't work either. Trips to the cleaners and grocery store, cleaning house, and other womanly duties sorta got in the way. How am I supposed to get slim if my whole world seems to work at taking my time to do everything else? But, every glimpse in the mirror urges me on. So, I trudge on and eat carrots like I love 'em.

I'm trying. The family thinks they have given up more for Lent than is fitting, but just like ex-smokers, we dieters have gotten an attitude. Label reading is quintessential, and we'll walk a mile for a no-fat cheese dip. Ah, the bridges we cross. I've been across this one before, but periodically running through one again doesn't hurt. The difference this time is I am not going to starve. There's no-fat ice cream and no-fat whipped topping!

Modern technology reigns! Maybe by next year at Mardi Gras, science will have developed the fat pill that will instantly take away all the calories from things like my mama's dressing or banana pudding, or cheese cake and king cakes. There would be cause for celebration!

Valentine's Day

Ah! Again, fast approaches Valentine's Day, and I drool and dream over the endless varieties of confections. I also promise myself out loud to go on a diet February 15. As I cruise the aisles, it amazes me how the different sorts of candy resemble the different types of love in my life.

Gooey candy reminds me of that first love I experienced as a student in the seventh grade at Dixon Junior High School. I shiver when I think of all the mush we wrote to each other, but it was wonderful then. We hated to part long enough to go to the bathroom at school, but heaven forbid, it does help me understand why ninth-graders relate to Romeo and Juliet.

Candy filled with a surprise inside rates right up there with the unpredictable discoveries of my teenage years through college. As I tried to discover myself, I searched for the perfect someone who would "complete" me and make me "fulfilled." Of course, it has taken me years to realize that completeness comes from being busy with the things that matter to you. And being happy with who and what you are. Happiness doesn't come from another person. Certainly, biting into that pleasantly tempting chocolate-covered morsel, and learning it has some weird orange middle I don't like, is as disappointing as learning some people are just as distasteful.

Then there are those little bags of pastel hearts with mushy phrases printed on them. It's fun to sift through the bunch and line them up to say what I want and in what order. I've attempted to line my life up in neat little categories. The only problem with that strategy is that someone usually comes along and rearranges everything. Sometimes I never get it straightened out. Children have a knack for re-ordering; so does government when they decide to go to war, or employers who move us hundreds of miles from our roots, or diseases that strike a change in our plans.

But perhaps the candy my daddy loves best should be the best example of Valentine's Day. He likes hard rock candy that lasts a long time, that he can carry in his pocket everywhere he goes, that is brightly colored and decorated. To me, rock candy is representative of my lasting, long-enduring, and long-loving family. They bring a sweetness to my life that I don't ever want to be without. I don't carry them in my pocket, but I do carry them in my heart. I never travel through a bridge without being aware of their surrounding love. In addition, Son, Sis, and Hon keep my bridges full of hugs, surprises, laughs, and loves.

What We Do For Love

The things a mom will do out of love for her family are endless. As I listened to my crew call out their questions and commands, I began to focus on the time-consuming task of being a caretaker.

"Mom, will you press this shirt for me?"

"Sweetheart, did you put up my favorite golf socks?"

"Hey, Momma Woman, what's for supper?"

You know, my resume would be very interesting if I were to cash in on the jobs. I don't think I will ever want a career that would take as many angles as motherhood, but you never know what a recession or time will bring. I could do laundry for a platoon, cruise ship, or a hospital after having done it for two healthy and involved teenagers. The mounds of towels, heaps of tee shirts, and mountains of jeans, not to count the stain control on tablecloths and the like, should qualify me for a Hilton. Then there is the job of short-order cook. It is not until everybody in the house is going to school, working, going to meetings, and on special diets that the American mom must don the apron of a fast food chef with a conscientiousness for fat molecules, the environment, the rain forest, and the ozone.

Son needs a good meal two hours before or after practice. Sis is on a diet; she wants nothing more than two calories on her plate no later than three p.m. (eating early is better for metabolism). Hon doesn't like vegetables and wants a good roast with potatoes and gravy. Me, do I get an opportunity to have quiet family time amid all this mayhem? Only in my recurring dream, where I am like Mrs. Cleaver and my kitchen floor shines like the marble halls of a museum.

Valentine's Day is a day of love, but I think my hat should be off to moms everywhere who love enough to do laundry at midnight, set alarm clocks to get up in the night to meet the bus at school after a field trip, hug weeping athletes after a hard loss, and weep themselves when filled with pride while watching one of their fledglings get a ribbon for reading the most books in the class.

Why do caretakers (moms, dads, grandparents, friends) make six stops to find just the right color pants, sit through endless recitals, or bake cookies? Love. We sometimes wearily tread across the bridge love builds, but we wouldn't miss the trip.

Map Reading

Right in the middle of the great state of California, a new revelation hit me. I now know why map makers sell so many road and city guides. Actually, there are several reasons.

Problem number one became obvious very quickly. After flying the friendly skies to save myself sanity and time, I found it necessary to rent a car and drive to most of the places I needed to be. Joe Rent-A-Wreck jingled the keys of a little red economy car and smiled an almost wicked sort of knowing smile. It didn't take long for me to understand the knowledge behind the grin. Traffic whizzed by me at 80 plus miles per hour, and I was lost. I suddenly wanted to be the navigator instead of the driver (a choice I would sooner than later regret).

I pulled into the nearest convenience store's parking lot and proceeded inside. A map would solve my problem. Umph! There were three maps of the area, so I decided to browse through the offerings in order to get the best one for the part of the state I would be traveling in the most.

I unfolded the first map, then decided it didn't suit the purpose. Problem number two arose. I could not fold the thing back like it was originally. I mumbled to myself and scanned the second map, then the third. By the time I had made it to the checkout counter, my frustration level was high and I purchased three unfolded maps. I lied and told the sales clerk I was doing a comparative study. I blushed, too embarrassed to admit I could not fold them back, and my mom had taught me not to leave a mess for someone else to clean up. Off I went at a horrendous pace, into traffic. Day and night, people sped past, and I cruised at 80 miles per hour.

Problem number three reared its ugly head. "What exit do I take to get to the civic center? The museum? What side of the interstate should I be on to get to the exhibit? How many blocks is it until I turn? Where do I go?"

This type of interrogation began every time I got into the car. I had flashbacks of two-year-olds, but problem number four brought me into the present. I could not see the print on the map. It had to be the size of a microscopic grain of sand. I adjusted distance, borrowed glasses, and cried as I attempted to decipher this grid of streets and names. Nothing helped. I got car sick to boot.

Never did I think to plot a course before getting into the car. Nor would I let go of my shopping money to buy a magnifying glass. Perhaps I should have searched for a copy of the city's layout in Braille. I suffered through eight days of frustrating bridges before I returned the tired, red flash to the rental service.

I'm going to write the Brotherhood of Map Makers in America and lodge a formal protest. Bigger print. I also think a big "X" with an arrow saying "You are here" should be placed on the thing before I walk out the store's door.

I will have to confess: I did not see the parks, personality, or landmarks of the cities I visited. The only memorable scene I have of the West Coast is the blur of blue, black, and red hazy stripes that were supposed to be a map. Truly, I was out of sight and out of mind!

Cleaning Closets

There are three things in my life that strike automatic terror in my heart: cleaning the refrigerator, cleaning the garage, and cleaning our closet. And there is no word adequate to describe the lengths to which I'll go to postpone and procrastinate. But I made a promise to Hon on New Year's Day that I would indeed clean the master closet before spring. Let me tell you, Hon didn't let an opportunity like that go to waste.

I had to sign my name in permanent ink on the calendar hanging in the kitchen for the entire family to view. "Don't want you to forget your promise. Wouldn't it be better if you just set aside a day and do it?" Hon coaxed me like a child, and, if looks could kill, I'd be collecting insurance money even as we speak. "Here, pick a day and I'll be sure to be at home to help you." There was no consolation in his voice.

I groaned and felt faint. "Thanks, but that's the last thing I need if I'm really going to do a good job in there." I pointed to the closet door with a gesture Moses could have used when parting the Red Sea.

The dramatics didn't help, and Hon handed me the calendar. "Pick and sign."

Reluctantly, I chose a Tuesday, in February, and all too quickly the dreaded day arrived. Having gone into training on the Sunday before, I practiced throwing out socks without mates and vacuuming a few baseboards and initiated a B-complex vitamin program.

"I've got to deliver these papers to...." I wasn't allowed to finish my sentence.

"It's Tuesday and you're stalling...." He recognized my *modus operandi*.

"Okay, okay. I'm going in there. Don't bother me." The cross tone of my voice was sufficient to ward off husbands, children, and pets.

I moved the portable TV inside so I could watch all the home improvement programs and commiserate with talk show guests. An idea came to me: What if Ricki Lake had a program on the prolonged effects of cleaning closets, then I could come "out of the closet," so to speak. The TV commentator blabbed on about how to redo a fireplace for less than $5,000.

Hours passed. The stacks of good, bad, and ugly stuff grew higher and higher. Boxes of scarves, belts, and bangles filled box after box to the brim. The decision-making process came a bit easier with the tossing away of each successive co-ordinating ensemble.

There. It's finished. The time on the digital clock glowed green: 1:30 a.m. Hey, and I haven't even eaten a snack. This closet cleaning deal might not be so bad, and it doesn't come around any more often than presidential elections. Yep, I won't have to cross this bridge again for four more years.

Peeking past the den door, I found Hon snoring contentedly in the lounge chair—remote control in one hand and a bag of pretzels in the other. His glasses dangled precariously.

"Well, you couldn't stay awake with me these hours to lend support to my mission, I see. But, hey, that's all right. I've got the entire experience on video tape," I said to my sleeping husband. I kissed him goodnight.

Spring Bridges

Winter is past, and spring bursts open like a brilliant daffodil in the warm sun. We plant with renewed hope and energy, take hope that the diets and cleaning will bring about lasting results, and examine our spirituality. Yes, these bridges of spring delight, surprise, and recharge the soul.

Slinky In My Dreams

I know it must be spring. Prom dresses are hanging on the racks of the department stores, and teenage girls are whipping around trying on every one in sight. Sis and I happened to see a fashion show of prom attire last week. She got all excited; I got all nervous.

As we viewed the first three models, one thing instantly struck me. Not one of them was as big around as my left leg. I tried not to exhibit my dismay, but Sis instantly picked up the change of mood.

"Mom, what's the matter? Aren't you having a good time? Which one of these full-length sequined gowns do you like?"

"I love the dark red one with the slit up the leg, but it looks like you would need to be at least twenty-five to wear it. The yellow one with the ruffles is cute, but who needs to dance all night with four inches of stuff around your nose and knees. I've never been one for fluff."

"Well, what about that deep purple one with the silver trim? Isn't it gorgeous?"

"You mean the one with no back to it?"

The model twirled by and I caught a glimpse of the price tag! "Four hundred dollars! I've never paid that for a complete wardrobe, much less for a dress with no back for a sixteen-year-old to wear for pictures and a few hours." I needed oxygen.

Another set of models pranced onto the runway. One was at least 5'7" and weighed 102 pounds. Another was so tiny it probably took only a yard of material for the dress. If I put on a gown that hugged my body that closely, I would exhibit enough moguls to make a high-class ski resort jealous.

"Never would my mom have let me out of the house in a black sequined outfit, even after I went to college. I borrowed one for a sophomore dance and got a lecture." I suddenly had flashbacks to my senior year at ole' Hometown High. Mom had my powder blue brocade and crepe dress made for about $40 and I felt like a queen. But, I broke out in chills as I contemplated what inflation could do in another year or two when we would be in the market seriously.

"These girls are fabulous! All the gowns are great!" Sis babbled. "I love all of them, don't you?"

"Sure, Sis, but I'm glad this is a bridge I can postpone for a little while longer. Maybe we should start a savings account for this today. And do me a favor. If I look like I'm daydreaming, just leave me alone. I'll be dancing to beautiful music in a blue slinky dress."

How My Garden Grows

I have spring fever big time! It hits me every year with a fury. Just as sure as the temperatures rise and the May days get longer, the urge to abandon schedules and the indoors grabs at my skirt and says, "Get outta the house!"

By the time this ultimatum of Mother Nature rules me, I have begun reading all the labels on all of the plants on every garden shop shelf. This type of shopping doesn't even bother Hon, for he figures pepper plants couldn't possibly grow in our closet. Early on, after perusing article after article, scouring picture after picture, visions of Martha Stewart-style patios and flowerbeds fill my head. I can rattle off the names of horticultural experts and columnists in as orderly a fashion as Son rattles NBA stars and coaches, and I'm able to spout off the scientific and common names of the shrubs, perennials, and annuals which are perfect for the Deep South. So what? you say. So can every amateur gardener worth their compost. And yet, I look back a generation and see something different.

My grandmother didn't buy bagged dirt. When she got ready to re-pot her ferns, she'd go out with a wheelbarrow and dig up some loamy woods dirt or dirt from the pastures. Her ferns, the size of a number three washtub, thrived while sitting on the shady front porch. Man, if she just knew that I buy pounds of non-fragrant, sterile poop, she'd huff and puff with indignation, and my ferns don't flourish nearly as well as hers did.

My mom has violets in every kind of pot, blooming like there is no tomorrow. I think I've got to have aeration and wicks and measure out the 7-7-7 plant food. And Dad—well, he just sticks stuff in the ground and it roots. His roses get pruned with loving care, but I'll bet he never reads about how to prune those little rascals so that the branches can breathe! He goes on instinct and experience.

Yes, there is a generation gap of sorts when it comes to gardening, but for me it is closing in fast. A phone call will harvest me the best advice on what to do with my sick bell peppers or cranky begonias. Practical experience is worth a lot and can save more greenery than all the printed words and lavish pictures.

My conversations with my folks are bridges connecting us to the mutual pleasures of a perfect tomato or a cluster of marigolds. Yes, and there are times when I truly feel the link and when we stop to share the smell of our roses. Ah, the fragrance is a treasure.

Address Book

"Hey, do you have cousin Mary's address?"

"Of course, Hon, it's in the address book with the green oriental print." Mumbling to myself as I give the kitchen counter a swipe, "It might as well be in Chinese if *you've* jotted in the entry."

"I thought we kept the book in the drawer under the phone."

"We did last year; now it's in the computer desk. Remember, we were going to move into the new century by getting all of our addresses on the label program. In your own words, 'We should be modern and up-to-date and use all this technology we've bought.'"

Hon groaned with the memory of recently trying to type into the computer the information of all of our friends and loved ones which we had accumulated over 30 years. It turned into a challenge for only the brave at heart with nerves of steel.

One of the first problems Hon encountered: sheer volume—three old address books and two Christmas lists full of names—hometown friends, kid's friends, family (always growing and changing), college buddies, colleagues, business folk. Add to the tangle the "yours, mine, ours" books. Actually, Hon displayed the patience of Job; however, to his dismay, I played the wifely supporting role by suggesting that he just give up the project and let it die. He didn't, so I may end up living with a man ranking right up there with a saint.

Another problem: handwriting and the deciphering thereof. Hon writes everything in his very own hieroglyphics with "h's" and "n's" and 12 other letters of the alphabet all too similar and equally illegible. Son copies down entries in dull pencil and phonetically, with total disregard for actual spelling. Sis's log-ins take two slots to record and she files them by first names—no last names appear. I'm not quite sure if that is to maintain entry anonymity, add to reader confusion, or is just a plot to botch up Hon's dream of the ultimate file in alphabetical order and organization.

Dealing with an unfamiliar computer program absorbed hour upon hour. When Hon finally declared the project finished and hit the print key, his eyes bulged wildly. The track-feed labels crunched and crumbled and the printer lights began to blink red. I shouldn't record the words and emotions of that moment.

In the end, not one of the old address books has been destroyed, and the dream of a volume with all the entries printed in uniform style is still a dream. That's okay, there's something warm and fuzzy about looking up the telephone number of an old friend in a book with edges well-worn by service. But, then there's my friend's e-mail address jotted in the margin. There may be a new turn to an old bridge.

Gone Buggy

A couple of ways to know that your children are definitely growing up is when they start using more hot water and towels than a metropolitan hospital laundry, your car leaves the garage more without you than with you, and your student is required to have an insect collection.

I can tell by the water bill that our little family has reached the first rung, but it wasn't until this summer that I realized that my baby was stepping toward the third rung. We have gone buggy at our house.

"You have to have fifty bugs! My goodness, that shouldn't be too difficult. Just sit outside late in the evening and you can get thousands."

"Mom, you don't understand." I always hate it when my children begin a discussion with those words. "Everything you see out there is not an insect."

"Oh, yeah! A bug is a bug."

"Wrong! Insects have six legs."

"You mean you've got to count the legs on these rascals? Well, if they have too many, just amputate until you have the right number."

Sis's eyes were wild. She could see before her the failure and humiliation of a classroom full of peers as the teacher pronounced her collection a fraud. "They also have to have all their wings and antenna."

So, in June, we set out like Noah to gather all the insects we could find. "Let's get two of everything just in case something happens. We might could even set up an insect swap shop," Sis suggested.

I imagined the deals being made..."I've got a green four-winged fly beetle. Whata you have to trade?" Oh, dear. I guess it's better than collecting reptiles.

I found myself carrying ziplock bags in my purse, having friends call to report a bug find, climbing on top of bookcases and cars to nab these creatures I had heretofore stepped on and squashed. As the summer waned, it soon became evident that catching insects was the easiest part of the assignment. But never fear, helpful advice on everything from catching to storage to presentation flowed from the more experienced friends.

"Mom, a friend told me we better stick the pins in these specimens while they're fresh. She also said to put them in the freezer for safe keeping. You know other bugs eat bugs." Family conversation had certainly deteriorated, even if the specimens had not.

"I can just see it now. Son will microwave the whole box of bugs before he opens the lid. Then he'll rant and rave about not having any supper. Or worse, what if a visitor opens my freezer to see pinned bugs instead of ice cubes." My heart rate went up ten points.

"Well, anybody that's had a kid in high school will know what's going on. We're supposed to use alcohol on a cotton ball to kill them quickly."

"Who? The bugs? The houseguest? Or me?" My question went unanswered.

As the summer months passed, the collection grew. So did our expertise at catching and preserving them. Of course, we had our mishaps and a few got soggy when left on the counter overnight, but our moths were exquisite. The most difficult part was yet to come—finding the scientific names for all these things! "Hand me that book. Do you think this bug looks like that bug?" My gaze was a bit haggard, as I handed over the guide.

Sis replied with an equal amount of stress: "No, but maybe we could paint and trim it to be close."

The assignment was met, and perhaps we crossed more bridges than we expected. We worked closely together, screamed, shouted, and laughed. We weren't too buggy after all.

D Day

Well, the time all mothers fear and all children dream of has come to pass in our family: Son's 16th birthday and the acquisition of a legal driver's license. There will never be another moment of peace in the house. Just about the time I got used to being the chauffeur, my job description changed to that of professional worrier for a teenage driver.

Along with that fact comes another amazing event: As if by magic, Son's legs stopped working. It will never matter if there is an oil crisis in the Middle East, or that he could walk a block and not have to get into the car, for, according to a commercial, and to Son, "It's not just a car; it's your freedom."

An example in point happened just hours after the wonderful "freedom card" had been issued by the state. "Got to go over to S.T.'s house and talk about geometry. I'll be back about seven." Son breezed past the door and grabbed a set of keys. This disturbed me. Three copies of the kitchen door key, all of which probably rest somewhere in the layers of mess in his room or in the pocket of jeans outgrown two years ago, will never be located without a massive search.

I begin praying that he keeps up with this set when I suddenly observe that he has not let go of the ring since he took the road test. He literally has his hands full. One fist grasps the remote control to the TV and the other folds around the car keys.

With dismay, I grumbled, "Be careful and drive slowly."

"Mom, I'm not gonna drive like some old grandpa! It'll ruin my image. I can't wait to try out my new speakers. They'll blast everybody out in the parking lot at the gym. See ya later."

"What *is* your image? Never mind, it would probably turn the rest of my hair gray. You will at least go to the grocery store for me, which will give the trip a little justification."

I am instantly seized by the fear that Son will not check the date on the milk or make sure the bread doesn't look like it is anything but crust, or that this bridge will be crossed at a speed beyond a comfortable 35 miles per hour. I will need lots and lots of coffee, but if he will relinquish the remote control, I'll manage the reruns of all the shows I've missed during my tenure as a taxi driver.

My Dream House

I'm no architect, but I am a mother-woman and I have a few ideas on what a dream house includes. I may lack the technical background to actually go to the drawing board, but, hey, life experiences and visions should count for something.

The first thing I would do is build a walk-in closet and bathroom for every member of the family. This closet would be large enough to hold not only the entire seasonal wardrobes of its owner, but also any sports and hobby equipment. For the children, the closet would also accommodate a washer, dryer, and an inexhaustable supply of clothes hangers (no clothes on the floor again). My dream of getting rid of the piles of dirty clothes my family generates would be taken care of with this feature, with the added plus of teaching everyone how to do their own laundry.

With each one's personal bedroom and bath facilities, I might as well put in a kitchen in their lock-away wing. But, no, to be honest and down to earth, it would really be cheaper to put them out on their own.

Windows and carpet should be self-cleaning in the modern homestead. A universal system sucking dust from the air should hum comfortably and constantly while also keeping the mold from the crevices of the tile in the bathrooms.

Another feature of my ideal house: a kitchen the size of two living rooms. In real life, everyone knows that no matter how pretty the living room, or how cozy the den, or how many guests are invited for dinner, the kitchen is the place people spend the most time in a house. Therefore, my fantastical kitchen should have large picture windows to see the birds and flowers, the sun and the rain; a fireplace by a big screen TV to enjoy all the sports programming; a dining room chair which could convert into a lounge chair so Hon could doze in comfort as I clean up the dishes; a computer center so the family could see that Son is still alive (although non-verbal) while locked into his favorite game or the internet; and a sink that would swallow up all the dirty dishes left in it for more than a couple of hours.

Next, the biggest major improvements would be in the garage. First, I'd design a 3,000-foot, two-car garage lined with cabinets and shelves from floor to ceiling. On one wall I'd have bins labeled: recycle, trash, yard sale. Speaking of yard sale items, I'd have a window with a drop-leaf shutter/table so I could instantly set up shop right from my bin! Of course, there would be generous storage space for Christmas stuff, yard stuff, and stuff that can never be thrown away. A Martha Stewart craft corner, complete with a plug-in for the glue gun, would be a must.

To round out my dream, the house would be surrounded with flowers blooming year-round (no weeds), and grass (the perfect height and the no-cut variety). There would be shade trees for the summer, fruit trees for the fall, and a garden spot for the spring.

Oh, well. This has been a fun bridge to dream my way across, but it's 4:00 p.m. and time to get back to reality. The laundry calls and dinner must be cooked!

Tee Off!

The game of golf is a fascinating and perplexing one. I've known adults to revert to childish tantrums and fits of near hysteria in what should be tranquil and inspiring surroundings. Therefore, I was not particularly happy when Son decided to fill up the seasons between football, basketball, and baseball with a golf ball.

"It's a lifetime sport, Mom." Son had obviously read the latest in health journals or sport magazines. The statement rang true in several respects. Golf is a game played on many different levels, and I concurred—to a point.

"Yes, I do agree with you. It is the only place a grown man is allowed to throw a metal object down and stomp like there is a national threat of wildfire. Or use language aloud normally reserved for locker rooms." My sardonic reply met inattention.

"Just think, I could be the next Arnold Palmer! Gulp, gulp, gulp, wham!" He devoured the sandwich and tea in record time.

"Probably so. You have about as much chance at that title as being another Arnold Schwarzenegger, but you do possess the perfect temperament for the game. You can sling and toss with the best, not to mention the truly invaluable experience you gained when you delved into closets, behind beds, and under couches just to find items needed to continue with our daily schedule of dressing and going to school. Oh, for sure, you are qualified in that area."

"Okay, I get the point. I think I'll use golf balls in those high-visibility colors—orange or yellow."

"Yeah, and the next pair of socks I buy will have high visibility stripes on them. That way, when you have to search in the bushes for your ball, your socks will match."

Son could tell that the conversation had degenerated into caustic clap-trap and he left—leaving me no bridge to cross.

Grazing

As I read one of my ladies' magazines Tuesday night, I came across a term which fit my children and the manner in which they watch television: "grazing."

Grazing is "extensive use of a remote control while very quickly reviewing all of the available cable channels." Let me explain in simple terms a mother can understand: See how fast you can flip from channel 2 to 98 before your mother faints. Now don't laugh too soon; this is a highly skilled art form. A viewer cannot rest longer than two seconds on any one station. But let me backtrack a little.

In December, my family purchased its first new TV in ten years. Great technological improvements have been made since 1979, and one is the remote control. Automatic combat zones were declared the moment the entertainment box was plugged in and seating territory claimed. Son, the biggest of the four of us, instantly won the first round and turned the assault to the tube, punching buttons faster than an accountant at tax time.

"Boy, this is great! I can watch three ball games at one time and keep up with the movie on 28." Son never heard any of the replies or complaints as he grazed past one channel after another. That in itself did not surprise me, since every man I know seems to want to be able to keep up with all the teams from coast to coast from season to season. "We need to order that magazine that tells what time everything on satellite comes on," he says.

"Well, it would encourage you to read more I guess. But, how is it that you can flip these buttons so deftly, yet you're the slowest thing with ten fingers in typing?" No reply, only the continuing change of channels. My eyes became tired, so I decided to go for a walk.

Trying to maintain avenues of communication within the family was difficult. I didn't even have the time between commercials to draw out a conversation.

Sis, who likes afternoon cable, seemed to be competing for a national prize in speed changing.

"What did you say, Mom? Hey, look, a rerun of 'The Cosby Show.' I just love all these old shows."

I gave up and went to my room, where I turned on the old TV without a remote control and brooded over the change in my children. What compelled them to race through program after program without ever seeing an entire episode from beginning to end? How would they ever know what cereal they are supposed to buy if they never see an advertisement?

A few days later, I sat alone in the den with the remote control in my right hand.

"Welcome to modern technology, Mom," Son interrupted as he reached for the little black box. He withdrew suddenly as I snapped more fiercely than a bulldog.

As I grazed, I found to my surprise the delight in being master of something that didn't have a smart remark for everything. Straightaway an impulse made my finger twitch as I fast forwarded through many programs and bridges. The virus had hit me!

Hear Ye

How is it my teenagers can understand the lyrics to all the current chart toppers, but can't hear the question I ask in a normal tone of voice?

"What did you say, Mom? The radio is up too loud."

"What, Mom? Hang on a second until I finish this round of scoring in Blaze Basketball."

"Do I hear the phone ringing? Wait a second. I'll answer it."

It is then that I usually raise the tone of voice to that of a rock star who shakes his head wildly, gestures with both hands for those already deaf, and twists in what seems to be real pain. The heads of both my children automatically turn.

"Gee, Mom, you didn't have to yell to get me to pick up my socks."

This cat and mouse game of attention had prepared me for the long waits I experienced when calling 800 numbers. The only difference: the businesses play sedate and soothing music, while my kids play the nervous jerk variety. Yet, even with all this preparation, I sometimes had my doubts about their ability to hear properly. I sprang into action.

Son had gotten so negligent in answering directly that I decided to have his hearing checked. As a younger child he had gone through the various ear infections. Rounds of doctor visits and tubes were common. I thought every child developed measles, chicken pox, colds, and ear infections. Those particular chapters in my Dr. Spock book were well marked. But, as time progressed, I became aware that I never got a direct answer to any question I asked. He seemed to be on another planet. So, I called the ENT doctor who hadn't seen Son since birth and made an appointment.

Donning earphones and looking like a contestant for a game show, Son sat in the glass booth for the hearing test. He would shake his head, look intently into space, mash buttons and the like. I nervously awaited the verdict following 30 minutes of this and that.

Now, it is always nice to see a doctor smile, but the pleasure of the announcement was short-lived. It dawned on me that if Son could indeed hear perfectly, why was I having to repeat myself so often?

The question has never been satisfactorily resolved, and the problem has become contagious. Sis appears to be more affected each day, but I don't think I'll go to the trouble to have her tested. Instead I'll put myself on video tape and do an instant replay, just like on the sports. Or, I'll find a bridge to bring a solution to this chronic problem.

Stuck Up!

My life must be one big example of Murphy's Law. If anything can go wrong or slow up a process, then by all means, it *will*. Case in point: Monday, I sat down at my computer. I had purchased one of those devices that stick to the top of the monitor and hold papers at eye level (I need all the help I can get with my typing). I pulled off the paper tabs and carefully placed the bracket to the left side of my screen. That should have been an easy task. Sure, but laws prevail.

I beamed with pride over the placement of my little gadget, and stuck my first paper in the holder and began to type. Everything seemed great. I didn't lose my place as much, my bifocals were reacting well to the levels of material and type, my desktop wasn't as cluttered, and there were no moving parts to break. What could go wrong? What a question.

As I clicked along, I began to notice a strange angle to the paper, one rather like a sinking sun, and my neck automatically adjusted. Hmm..., this page is tilted. Wonder why? Investigating, I discovered the glue on the bracket must have been weak. The right edge of the contraption listed badly. But I can solve this problem. I'll just stick it myself with my own glue.

Some things are banned in my house, and superglue should be at the top of the list. After my fingernail experience, one would hope I had learned a valuable lesson, but I'm a slow learner.

This little white bottle had the "new design." That ought to help me out. There's a pin in the top to keep it from getting clogged. This shouldn't take but a minute, but these directions are in microscopic print. I put glue on one side of the bracket and counted up to 15 very slowly. Then, the miracle was supposed to happen, but Murphy's Law intervened instead. The bracket did not hold—it swayed, then dropped to the desk. Must not have done that right. I'll put more glue on this side and try again.

Some of the stuff oozed out of the cracks, and instinctively I swiped it up. Instantly, my thumb and forefinger bonded. My fingernails stuck to the skin behind them. While trying to pull my fingers apart, the apparatus on the monitor clattered atop the yellow legal pad on my left. Why is it I can stick anything but what I want together? Maybe I should appear as if I am giving an okay sign to everything rather than take off three layers of skin. No, the kids would really take advantage of me. Okay, this is going to hurt, but.... I yanked the fingers apart and tears welled up in my eyes. I should get a hammer after this thing, or sue. It is false advertising to state that this object will stick anywhere and this glue will hold a transfer truck up with a matchbook-size patch of glue.

The sad ending to the story is that I took clear plastic mailing tape and placed three strips across the back of the bracket atop the monitor. It now has the appearance of something from a war zone—not a clean, efficient, modern office.

I refuse to go through this bridge again. Twice is enough. In a third adventure, I would probably glue my armpits or lips together. Well, my pasta is the only thing I have that would stick anywhere. Hey, maybe I should put spaghetti noodles on my monitor. They would drape nicely.

Lights Out!

"Hey, Momma Woman! Me need light bulb for cave. Heap big black hole," Son yelled. I pointed the way to the cabinet.

"Me, too! My lamp's shot and I can't read the covers of the CD's," Sis added.

"What's going on?" I wondered aloud. "This is the third or fourth bulb I've put in a socket since vacation. Surely some little devil didn't sneak in with a little hammer and zap all my lights, did they?" I dismissed the thought and headed for the cupboard storing the light bulbs. Several days passed without incident.

Then, just like in the paperback novels, it happened. "It was a dark and stormy night...." I had gotten caught in a sudden thunderstorm while in town shopping for groceries. I pulled into the carport and grabbed a bag as I pushed my keys into the lock. Struggling to reach the switch, I dropped my heavy bag filled with all my canned goods specials. It never fails. Well, at least I'm dry and this wasn't the bag with the eggs in it. I should have estimated my luck afterwards.

I flipped the switch, but the light didn't come on. Instead, out shot this little spark of blue lightning into the dark room. All was silent. Son, gone off to eat with his buddies, probably wouldn't be home for hours. Sis was spending the night with a gaggle of giggling girls. Hon had a meeting in town. I was alone with a car to unload and a murky room. Thank goodness for the coffeepot light and the lamp one of my forgetful children left burning in the den.

About the time I had made my third trip to the car, Son wheeled into the driveway. "Just in the nick of time," I whispered to myself.

"Mom, what are you doing? Don't you think it's kinda weird to be putting up stuff in the dark?"

"Oh, you're just in time. Need you to replace this light." Usually, my requests for help are met with moans and excuses, but this was big business. If the kitchen were to remain dim, he would have trouble locating all the glasses, snacks, and drinks for his nightly foraging. Some blessings are in disguise.

Another week went by before the next rash of blowouts hit. This time, the blight came to the bathroom. I raced around in a hurry, as always. My meeting began at 7:00 a.m., and it was 6:45. Swirling around the corner into the bathroom, I automatically reached to turn on the Hollywood-style lights. Two out of the top four "pinged" and darkened.

As I tromped once more to the storage cabinet to snatch replacements, I mumbled disquieting comments under my breath. "I should own stock in GE. Never in my life have I had so many disruption...." I stopped mid-sentence and stared in disbelief. There were no spares! "It's got to be a communist plot. They plan to attack from Cuba under cover of darkness." I arrived late to my meeting and had a rather disheveled air about me.

I determined to store up a light bulb for every fixture in the house and to never cross this dark and lonely bridge again. Besides, climbing all those stepstools could be dangerous to my health!

Battle Of The Sections

I am not a picky person about most things in my life. I drink from the same coffee cup for three weeks in a row at work. I don't iron my sheets, nor do I have to have all my glasses in the cupboard arranged by color and in neat little rows. But I *do* have to read my newspaper from front to back with all the sections in order.

I suppose a psychiatrist would have a field day analyzing why so much of my life is in disarray, and yet this one area must be just so. I can't recall anything from my childhood that would cause me to have such a steadfast rule about my paper-reading habits, unless it is the fact that I have short arms. I didn't have a great Aunt Susie who yelled and screamed until everything passed the white glove inspection, nor was I beaten if I pulled the comics out before reading the editorial letters.

For whatever reason I acquired this habit, my children and spouse have not; hence, the battle for the sections begins the moment the paper is picked up out of the mailbox. If I am lucky enough to be the first one to grab the paper, I head immediately for the kitchen table or the living room floor (whichever has the most cleared and uninterrupted space) to spread the news before me. This gives me the opportunity to leaf through the pages and scan them from top to bottom with quick or lingering glances.

Some days I am not so fortunate, and finding all the parts to the paper is like participating in a scavenger hunt. Son takes the sports pages and disappears. Sis wants to see the clothes ads and school section and grabs them as if she has only ten seconds to do so or she will be transformed into a glob of slime. Mysteriously, the recipes float toward the kitchen counter or close to the microwave. The kids think I'll take the hint and try all these dishes with 10,000 calories a bite and which take three hours to prepare. Hon loves the front page, the classified ads, and the comics in random order. After the three of them finish with the latest edition, it takes me 20 minutes to reassemble all the stray parts, but it's worth it.

There is something very comforting and civilized about being able to browse through each piece of news and pause to read whatever catches my fancy about world events. I can grumble about meat prices, clip wedding, birth, and death announcements (I mail them to friends and family far away, or carefully paste them into an album which will be a bridge of record for generations to come), or to muse at the cycle of life so publicly recorded. It sorta makes me feel like the stage manager in Thornton Wilder's *Our Town*. What a shame, the drama simply written in daily episodes of real life—and too true to life—is often so carelessly scattered.

Wishing On A Star

One of the first little rhymes I taught my children was "Star light, star bright, first star..." along with the rules of wishing. "Remember, when you wish, you can't tell what it is you wished for." Of course, Son, (a chain talker), would burst if he couldn't tell what it was he dreamed of in the silence of his imagination, so he would blurt out his request. This would always bring a hail of comments from everyone standing around, and little Sis would blink her big baby blues and realize that brother had done something outrageous—again.

As I have gazed into the early night sky over the years, I have wished for thousands of things complicated, impossible, and simplistic. Once, as a child, I asked for my front teeth to come in, and they did, a month later. I have also yearned for peace on earth and for all hungry children to be fed. So, even though I can't testify to the true magic of star wishing, I am still actively engaged in the ritual.

Driving from the post office last evening, I spied the first star of the night, brightly glowing in the pink sky. Taking a deep breath, I made my wish. Maybe it was because I sat alone with no telephones ringing, no one wanting supper right that instant, that for a brief second, all schedules were pushed aside. However, this particular night, as I continued to drive, I discovered that my star was moving! I blinked my eyes, adjusted my glasses, and tried to focus on the light. And then *it* blinked, not me!

Much to my chagrin, I had not wished on a star or even a planet—it was a small plane. I felt so cheated that I didn't even search for the real "first star" to re-do my request. I just pulled into the driveway and sat with a sour expression on my face.

Sis bounced out of the kitchen door to check on me. "Are you okay, Mom? You look sorta mad."

I didn't respond to her; I just shook my head and climbed out of the car. "You know, I think there needs to be a new endangered list started for stars," I mumbled. She appeared puzzled, but took the mail from my hands. "I hate to feel cheated, and tonight I was tricked while making a most important wish. It was some UFO moving at an undetermined speed."

Son, my own personal UFO, whizzed by, then turned to speak as he opened the refrigerator. "Mom, we're studying space in science these days. Do you think there's life on another planet or in another galaxy?" (It amazes me yet that all this scholarly wisdom can be delivered while pouring the last quart of milk in the house into a jelly glass.)

"I don't know. Wait a minute, maybe these beings from another world inhabit my wishing star and have decided to drive right past my windshield." The children eyed each other and began howling with laughter.

"I love you, Mom, but sometimes you're weird," pronounced Son, as he began gulping milk.

I didn't even respond to his common insult. I was already bridging this event of disillusionment and pondering whatever might be the next. I'm sure I felt rather like Daniel Boone must have when he saw the smoke curling up from his new neighbor's cabin. Civilization must be closing in, except this time, where do we move? The nearest wishing star?

Nightmare On Express Lane

The inventor of the 12 Items or Less/Cash Only lines in stores must also write horror films and be a demon straight from the flames of purgatory. This devil, knowing and understanding enough about modern society, tempts and tests until an average person can be transformed into a monster using language unacceptable to mothers and most sailors.

Getting out of a store in two or three minutes should not be a practical joke, and I am always enticed into the express lane hoping this time will be different from all the others. But, as I plunder through my purse, the discovery that I am a dollar shy of the cash amount threatens my dream. Faced with evaluating how desperately I need the item or finding a new line in which to stand, the idea of how anybody ever has enough cash for eight or ten purchases in these days of blue light and unadvertised specials wanders into my brain. I also ponder why the sign allows only 12. Why not 10 or 15? Why is 12 magic?

On one occasion, I rushed into line with a single pie shell. I had five minutes before dinner company was to ring my doorbell. Running into the express line, I spied only one little woman perched at the counter. But, as I stopped, a closer look horrified me. She had a basket full of stuff!

"Lady, you're supposed to have fewer than 12 things," the young clerk explained in a controlled and quiet voice.

"Oh, I do. I'm buying for me and my neighbor who couldn't come to the store today. Her daughter from Florida...." The explanation faded as the sales clerk began to have flashbacks of his childhood and the authoritative rebukes his grandmother gave. With the problem sort of cleared and the groceries registered with two separate amounts, the lady announced, "I want to pay you with this check." She then flipped out a pre-written check for an amount much larger than the total bill. The young man at the register began to have sweaty palms as he called for the manager and patiently tried to explain the store policy of cash only in the express lane.

Meanwhile, the line behind me multiplied as we were all shuffling our feet and glaring at wrist watches as if we were choreographed. Multitudes of people pushing buggies brimful of merchandise in aisles next to the express lane were checked out, bagged, and gone as I stood my turn. The demon probably chuckled.

With my pie crust softening, one consolation came to me. I would not have to use the microwave to thaw it—it had *already* thawed. The little shopper in front of me waited for her check to be cleared, and about the time I thought everything was about to break loose like the spring thaw in Canada, she leaned past me to snatch the latest tabloid splattered with stories of aliens, Liz Taylor, and O.J.

"How much is this? It is only one item." She glanced at me over her glasses with the daresome look mothers give children contemplating trouble. "Never mind, I'll take it." She did pay cash this time, but she complained with strong adjectives to the boy about the cost.

I stepped to the counter, and the clerk breathed a deep sigh of relief. I had cash and one product. Rushing out the electric doors and through the bridge home, I vowed never to use the express lane unless there was absolutely no one in line. I'll bet the inventor just sits somewhere and laughs aloud awaiting the sequel: "Express Lane II."

Easter Hunt

Egg hunts have long been an Easter tradition in our family. The entire brood gathers on the front lawn and literally puts all the eggs in one basket. Three adults count, and one would think the final results would be the same. Not so. Somebody always has to be interrupted or go to the bathroom. So, one year the official count was recorded to help verify the final tally. There are sometimes up to 50 real and plastic eggs, with one prize egg. Grandmother has sweetened the booty in recent years by putting quarters, gum, or small toys in all the plastic eggs.

Our clan has two divisions of egg hunts. One is the beginners' competition, and a participant can graduate out of the league by proving to have expertise in finding a basket full of eggs quickly. I am still with the beginners. In this round, the eggs are placed on top of tables, in front of rocks, and at safe distances from flower beds. The yard usually looks like it has hailed multitudes of pastel drops. Right out in the open, a little kid can find as many as ten eggs. The nice part about this round is that the munchkins don't realize the eggs are not really hidden, and for the peace of the entire family, the contest is repeated several times or until each has a full basket, and a prize.

Then, the real business of hiding eggs in the masters' round starts. The participants are sequestered in a place where they cannot possibly see outside. The curtains are drawn and a monitor is put in charge. Meantime, outside, Mom and one of my brothers stash the booty.

Now, these folks have taken lessons on egg hiding from my Uncle W.D., the toughest egg hider this side of the Rockies. When the splash of kids come out the den door, there is not an egg in sight, nor is there a clue on the faces of the official hiders. Eggs are discovered in drain pipes, under several inches of straw, behind shutters, or inside the barbecue grill. Mom once put one in her apron pocket. The kids almost never discovered that one.

A standing rule is that, once a certain number of eggs have been found and the search party seems to be stumped, clues of "hot or cold" are allowed. The best spot the committee ever placed an egg was under Dad's hat! He sat there at the picnic table as solemn as a judge. The hints were given, but finally, instead of an egg cracking, Dad cracked a grin and helped one of the little ones tip his tat. Half the crew was delighted, the other half pouted.

There have been years when snow or rain forced the hunt into the den, and there have been transitions from real grade A large to plastic, but the hunt goes on. And as each generation holds the hand of the new one, they become the bridges our family builds onto itself with the guidance of experience and the exuberance of youth.

Cold War

The cold war is on at the Fletcher house! Territory is being staked out daily and threats are being made! No, it's not land, not money, not even space. It's food! And fight'n words can be heard at all hours of the day when terrain has been violated.

I shop for groceries about once a week and try to stock the pantry and fridge with staples and some goodies. Most are for the entire family, but a few items are purchased with certain dinners or people in mind. Moms around the world pride themselves in pampering their brood with favorite foods. I buy creamy peanut butter because Sis and Hon don't like crunchy. I get a loaf of white bread for Son (who has refused since the age of five to eat wheat bread), and a loaf of special bread for the rest of us. I buy fresh veggies for me and a natural vanilla ice cream for Hon. And that's where the most recent war began.

Hon tooled into the kitchen late Tuesday afternoon. He whistled his favorite tune as he swung open the freezer door. "Think I'll have a bowl of ice cream to tide me over until supper." His head poked in, then he dove a little farther, but his words were lost in the hum of the machine trying to compensate for all the cold air rushing out. Rustling of boxes and containers muffled his string of comments, and then he sprang back out of the freezer as if he had been zapped. Indeed, he had been zapped.

"The ice cream is gone!"

I disregarded his comment; he can't usually find a fork on the table without a loran. "Hon, it's got to be in there somewhere. I just bought a gallon two days ago. And brush the frost off your eyebrows."

"It's not here." He skulked away into the den to watch the golf match. I opened the freezer just to check it out for myself. No ice cream. The answer was simple to me—Son and Sis. For years my children have had the habits of mice: Attack at night!

I have gone to bed many a night thinking all was well provided for, and have gotten a shock when I opened the fridge door the next morning to see the havoc of a midnight raid. After several "company items" disappeared, and empty cartons of ice cream and milk were left as spoils of war, I launched a campaign to label and identify foods not cleared for general consumption.

My carrot sticks (all washed and ready for my lunch bag) have my name taped to them. The vanilla ice cream has Hon's; Sis has tagged her diet drinks. The pizza ranch dressing belongs to Son and Son alone—nobody else in the clan will touch it; therefore, it needs no label. The war is on. Territories are infringed, mistakes are made, and woe be unto the soul who has eaten the ears off the chocolate Easter rabbit and then carefully wrapped it back up and disappeared! I'll find you if I have to fingerprint my hare!

This bridge is still under siege. The general of the kitchen will win!

Procrastination Pros

I should have christened my oldest: Son Wait-A-Minute-Mother Fletcher. He, along with his sibling, has practiced the terrifying art of procrastination at its highest level.

The most recent episode came this week when both children had major projects due on Wednesday. The need to get busy and finish these tasks did not become a revelation from God until 6 p.m. Tuesday, even though outlines and requirements, topics and resources had been gathered weeks ago.

"Mom, I've got a basketball game in 45 minutes. Will you type this paragraph for me?" Sis blinked her baby blues like an orphan child in a silent film, so I haltingly agreed and sat down to type. "I'll need to get my uniform out of the dryer, so I'll put another load in." Sis obviously understood the house rule of "help and be helped," so I nodded.

But upon glancing at the paragraph, I erupted faster than Mount St. Helen. "This is barely legible! How am I supposed to make sense of this?"

"It doesn't matter right now anyway, Mom. We gotta go to the game or we'll be late!" Sis snatched keys and a coke as she broke all Olympic track records to dash out the kitchen door. I sat in disbelief only for a second. For even as I sat, Son, as busy and subversive as any Central American revolutionary, began stacking books by the word processor and commanded possession of the territory. I surrendered on the spot.

The game was played; time passed. Upon return, Sis acted like Cinderella. The hour had come to return to the kitchen. We found Son typing away more frantically than a legal secretary in a fire.

"I'm not finished with this yet, so you'll have to wait your turn," Son proclaimed. Astonishment spilled into Sis's and my faces.

"What have you been doing all this time?" Our duet was in strained, high tones.

"Well, ESPN covered the west coast finals and they're just now over," spoke he in such a matter-of-fact tone that we almost accepted the statement. But before I could count to three, war broke out with a fury.

I can't record the violence and rage of the next few hours. At 11:30 p.m., and after cutting out multicolored letters from construction paper, I announced my retirement. "I'm going to bed."

"But, Mom," said Sis-But-Mom-Fletcher, "what am I going to do?"

"Beats me." I closed my bedroom door on the holocaust of papers, staples, trifolds, and kids. An eerie silence fell.

I don't know what transpired after that. The next morning, as I meandered through the cold confusion of supplies, I spotted two rather presentable projects sparkling in the sunlight. I felt as if Christmas had arrived early. The elves had worked all night on the final touches, and miracles had been wrought. "Maybe, just maybe," I muttered to myself, "those little imps will want to cross this bridge a different way next year." But, then again, maybe this is the Twilight Zone.

Chocolate Covered Easter

I have a dear friend who every year gives up chocolate for Lent. She's a sweet lady for 11 months, yea, a virtual angel, but verily I say unto you, she's as wired as a momma bear waking from hibernation after a winter without honey!

This petite, smiling blondie changes as drastically as Dr. Jekyll to Mr. Hyde. As her neighbor, I can keep my phone calls to a minimum and buy my own sugar instead of borrowing, but her family faces a different situation. Case in point: Do you know how many commercials there are on TV showing chocolate dripping over everything from almonds to cornflakes? Gazillions. The sad part is, on a 30-inch screen, even the mini-sized Snickers or Milky Way appears to be the size of Delaware. The groans and sighs of pain pierce kitchen walls, so in order to drown out her pitiful cries, I gobble and crunch on another handful of pink M & M's.

She can't even escape in the car. The radio spills out special sale ads for Dairy Queen's peanut buster, McDonald's hot fudge sundae, and TCBY's fat-free chocolate yogurt. Don't even mention the grocery store or Wally World. The aisles burgeon with rabbits, eggs, baskets, carrots, and chicks, in dark, white, milk, real, and fake chocolate. The bakery section becomes a torture chamber with rows of chocolate covered doughnuts, fresh and fragrant, lining the shelves.

Reading offers only a small retreat. Even there, all the magazines print recipes for double Dutch chocolate cakes, or ways to bake chocolate chip cookies with rabbit ears and whiskers. Their covers flaunt titles of strange articles like the one for the World Bazaar, "Woman Eats 300 Pounds of Chocolate Before Alien Takes Her Away."

Truly, Lent is a period of prayer. My dear neighbor prays diligently, although I don't think all the prayers are supposed to be for strength to keep her commitment. And indeed, the biggest test for her during this interval between Valentine's Day and Easter is the arrival of a case of Thin Mint Girl Scout cookies delivered annually by her granddaughter. Even the UPS man smells like minty chocolate! It's almost more than a mortal should have to bear.

I have a present for her for Easter sunrise: chocolate covered cherries (her absolute favorite treat) shaped like Easter eggs—in a chocolate basket. If I could find chocolate straw, I'd put that in too, but I would probably need to give her first aid if I did that. I respect the yearly bridge of faith and commitment she crosses, but I gotta stay out of her way come Easter morning. Bears are mighty mean just coming out of hibernation.

A Type "A+" Mother

Moms come in all shapes and sizes, and I feel like I am qualified to make a few observations on motherhood since I personally have known and loved thousands. Being a mother myself lends truckloads of understanding to these women of our world who struggle to balance everything from hormones to checkbooks.

One type of mother found in modern society is dubbed "Cleaning Woman." This creature produces astounding, sparkling, and anti-fungal feats. She can get up at five in the morning, cook pancakes for her brood, and serve them with syrup bottles that don't stick to the hand or placemat. She can have the floors mopped in the kitchen and bathrooms by seven. What does she do the rest of the day? Well, silly, she bakes fresh bread for dinner, and gets all of her laundry either folded and put away or ironed and hung up. I really don't have a clue about what she does with her stationary bike, but I have not been the only mother I know to invent the chrome clothes hanger (also know as modern bedroom sculpture with a personal touch).

Then there is the "Athletic Mom." She runs five miles a day in addition to the miles she travels after toddlers, to and from errands, and between ballfields. She can pitch a ball to the child practicing for the little league team, catch the one thrown by a wild outfielder, and keep the ball rolling on the playground project the parent association passed to her in the last meeting. I admire her. I almost got brain damage helping Son learn to play baseball, and had multiple bruises helping Sis bounce basketballs in the back yard. The president of the parents' organization skillfully made me a part of the pick-up crew rather than risk a physical and emotional injury. I hate this woman. She still looks good in her slightly tight jeans and tee shirt. She has a cute, youthful stroll. My jeans are tight, but I'll never divulge the size I buy, and my stroll is more of a waddle.

My favorite type of mom is friend I grew to appreciate and love with each experience of my life. She can repair toilets and TVs, dump trucks and dolls. The tool kit in the house is pink—it belongs to her. She can do a roast and vegetable soup with the best of them, although her culinary claim to fame is banana pudding by the washtub and biscuits by the dozen. Her hands create music, painting, bouquets, and padded satin stitch, and still have time to comfort, even from three hundred miles away. And, hey, she's *my* mom, a true "A+" kinda mom.

Here's wishing all the moms out there a Happy Mother's Day!

Summer Bridges

Ah!! The bridges of summer make us feel as carefree and lazy as Huck Finn. Fishing poles dangle from our shoulders, and the chirping of the cricket songs welcome our ears as we traipse barefoot through the sand and the mud of the riverbanks. There is always the temptation to linger. Ah, summer!

Ah! Vacation

My, how quickly a year can pass and vacation time come again. I don't really know why I should call it vacation, for, when 15 family folks, ranging in age from nine months to retirement, choose to spend a week together by the seashore, relaxation is at a premium.

The shoreside house appeared large enough to meet our needs—plenty of beds and bathrooms, a big kitchen with pots and dishes, a swing, and some shade. The clan had not stretched out in the beach chairs in the sand long when everyone realized that the youngest of the bunch hailed from a different time zone and his nap and eating habits would never conform to the rest of ours. Case in point: At four a.m., baby wanted breakfast and playtime, which proved to be about the time the teenagers crawled into bed from all-night video and music vigils. They did not rise again until four p.m. Weary-eyed adults struggled to nap and cope.

Meals wreaked havoc and bore the semblance of a school cafeteria during peak serving time. When I grew up, the adults got to eat first, but I discovered that times have changed. Although everything was served from the counter, those little guys and gals in the front of the line spilled half their servings and the teenagers devoured unbelievable quantities, leaving foods in total disarray likened to a war zone. It would certainly make Martha Stewart nauseous to see our presentation.

We did assign the cooking to mixed groups of aunts, uncles, and kids. No child cooked with his own folks, and the chefs did not clean. The night Son and his uncle had to cook for the gang, I broke out in a sweat and decided to take my new book to the swing and disregard all the questions and howls coming from the stove. Only two people escaped kitchen detail, my dad and the baby. Neither would have been any help, so instead of whipping up salad or hot dogs, each drew the assignment of entertaining the other.

On deck, the conversation flowed unhurriedly, while underneath, in the cool, shaded sand, the smaller children sang, played make-believe, and built castles. The brothers and mothers caught up with the goings and comings of our big, changing family. The ocean roared in the background and transported us away from our everyday struggles to a different universe where no one wore shoes or watches. We drank enough coffee to keep Juan Valdez in business, and walked miles of sugar-soft shores.

It amazes me that we manage to find a week when all of us can gather, which is all any of us seem to be able to spare from jobs, practices, and duties binding us to churches, schools, homes, and teams. But I heard each exclaim 'ere they drove out of sight, "Check your e-mail for next year's date—we'll call you tonight!"

Suiting Myself

If I see another article defining which swim suit I should purchase to look taller, younger, or thinner, I may throw up in my bowl of chocolate Blue Bell ice cream. It seems as if every publication from January to June carries a cover story about bathing suits. I try so hard not to confront this issue, but alas, every time I stand in line at the grocery store, I am bombarded with ideas and illustrations.

Now, dear friends and loved ones, in all our years of buying magazines and reading newspapers, I ask you, has there ever been a photo of a model with my body type? No! Yet, I vividly recall a report I read defining the different body types—you know—with terms like mesomorph and endomorph. The article included a paragraph of explanation and the name of a film star with that particular body type. I perused the information and concluded I matched the definition of the body type given to actress Elizabeth Taylor. Not long thereafter, I needed a physical to apply for a job. My family doctor, who had known me all of my life, was checking my ears. I informed him of my mesomorphic discovery. The doctor coughed as if choked and then gulped in amazement. He could not make a verbal reply. He spoke with my mother in private.

Ever since that reaction, I refrain from disclosing such information. Current articles continue to parade models who are at least 5'9", pushing up a bustline like that of a *Playboy* centerfold, and touting long blonde hair while dripping sparkling droplets of water and kicking up her high heels on some rock on an exotic island. The average reader gawks, for she is a middle-aged mother who can't imagine wearing five-inch taupe heels with a

Sunday dress, much less with a bathing suit that has no more material than a placemat!

The modern woman suffers through the whims and declarations of fashion, but I'm here to tell you that designers can put stripes vertically *only* on my couch and blinds. Recently, when I tried on a suit with vertical stripes, Sis, my true and vocal critic, reeled in nausea and dashed for the bathroom. One season, my cut-away suit left me with a pieced-up tan line similar to the lines of Frankenstein monster's face. And the suit with the French cut legs—it was never seen in public.

Every spring I vow not to worry about what I look like in a swim suit, and every spring when on the beach next to a 5'9" blonde with a crocheted bikini, I curl up in my chair and hide behind my paperback novel with the attitude of a matron in a black and white English mystery.

But, I escape on the bridge of fantasy and envision the gal next to me seven months pregnant, having two sets of twins, and definitely not looking like Christy Brinkley at 40! Revenge is sweet in any form.

Survival On Hwy 59

Hon just doesn't understand time management sometimes, and the male trait of traffic impatience rose to an angry surface every time he got into his car this past week. I really felt that I must help him learn to cope with the 20- to 30-minute, three-mile drive down Highway 59, so I proceeded to write a list of useful ideas and posted it on the dash of his car Wednesday morning.

Wednesday afternoon, he came rolling into the kitchen with my agenda in his raised hands. Wild-eyed and dazed from the grueling drive, he flapped my note in the air.

"What in the world is this?"

"Thought I'd give you some pointers on using your time wisely while in such awful traffic. All you have to do is be prepared." My voice had that pseudo-calm tone that I learned from listening to all those 1-800 help operators.

"I'm not putting a basket of magazines and a cooler filled with fat-free yogurt in my front seat!"

"Okay, so you don't like that idea. What about the Tolstoy novel and John Jakes' series in the backseat? Really, Hon, I thought you'd like number five: Balance the checkbook."

"It's better, but number two: Open the sunroof and work on my tan? If I did that I would burn my bald head!"

"That's what the sunscreen in your all-purpose kit is for, silly. You know you could write your son a letter, or make a list of all the sizes of ziplock bags we need, using the pen and paper from your kit. Well, it was just intended to ease your troubled spirit and keep the cellular phone bill smaller than the house payment."

"Thanks. I've found one consolation in all of this."

"Oh?"

"Yeah, you don't get out and shop as much since it takes so long to get anywhere, and you've started growing your own fresh veggies."

"I know. It's sad when I've been reduced to learning all the words to the tapes the children have left in the car, and letting my clothes go out of fashion while trying to make it to the grocery."

"Well, darlin', this is only a temporary detour for this bridge. We'll both make it through. Hey, what's for dinner anyway?"

"Oh, we're not going out?"

Hon raised the list in the air and shook his head. "Not even if I'm reduced to no-fat cheese and bean sprouts."

Stiff Stuff

If you see me in my flowered cotton sundress, shining like a kitchen sink, then you'll understand why I gave up aerosol products for reasons other than the ozone layer. The afternoon I sprayed my dress with kitchen and glass cleaner instead of spray starch, Sis giggled all the way back to her jingling phone.

Now, I've had trouble with aerosols since my early college days. One of the worst episodes occurred during my sophomore year. I had quickly showered in order to get to the homecoming festivities already in high swing. I thought I reached for the deodorant, but instead I grabbed my extra-hold hair spray bottle. Instantly, my right underarm took a solid stance and I knew how Lady Liberty kept her torch high. As I lowered my arm, the crinkling of skin could be heard all the way down the hall, and I headed for the shower—again.

That incident seemed to set the tone for other such embarrassing events. But, I thought I had managed to outgrow them until Wednesday night when I started to press my 100 percent cotton dress. Cotton may be the fabric of our lives, so I won't get on my soapbox about everything hanging in the stores being permanently wrinkled instead of permanently pressed, nor will I try to explain how my kitchen cleaner managed to get onto the ironing board of my laundry room. Just use your imagination and then add the fact that two teenagers live in my house.

Feeling really domestic as I stood at the ironing board ready to do battle with the shirts and skirts of natural fabrics, I sprayed a good dose of what I thought was starch onto the skirt of the flowered dress. When the material didn't press the way I thought it should, I squirted again.

Suddenly, the front of the label was turned upward and "All Purpose Cleaner" glared at me. I couldn't believe it. I had done it again!

Sis heard me grumbling and peered in to see about me. "What's the matter? Oh, you found the sink cleaner. I looked everywhere for it the day you left me in charge of kitchen duty."

I glowered and continued to grumble. "Wish I'd seen the label two sprays ago. Now I'll have to wash this dress again or pretend that my cologne is Eau de Kitchen." Sis retreated to her room feeling as if she had viewed a sitcom of a mentally disturbed woman instead of her real world.

Oh well, this bridge I cross will not only have plenty of body, but will be germ free to boot! I picked up the next piece to be ironed, and read the label carefully this time.

There Are Some Days

There are days when my elevator doesn't run all the way up to the top and I blame the really dumb things I do on being short, the moon and tides, bio-rhythms, *anything* that might help explain away the incidences. To add to my frustration, I usually have an audience.

You'd think plunking a stamp onto an envelope addressed to my dear Auntie would be brainless. I tore the stamp off the roll, licked it, placed it in the right corner, and it didn't stick. I tried another, then another, each buckled and stubbornly refused to stick.

So, last Tuesday at the post office, I patiently stood in line behind three people and in front of four, until I managed to perform my Ralph Nadar impersonation and explain to the worker that my six dollar roll of stamps didn't work.

She examined the merchandise, then peered over her spectacles, grinned, and cleared her throat. "Lady, there's nothing wrong with these. They are peel-off stamps."

I felt like the kid in the jokes who misses her mouth with the ice cream cone only to hit her forehead. Duh. And there were four people behind me snickering.

Then, the same week, I planned to fill up the car at one of the new computerized gas pumps. I read the instructions and inserted my faithful credit card. The screen blinked back, "Error, re-insert card." After the third try, I studied the pictures. Shoot, I had it in backwards! The guy at the other pump gave me this "lady you should stay at home" look.

Both of these incidents don't measure up to what I named "My Most Embarrassing Moment." On a foreign field north of the Mason-Dixon

Line, I anxiously paused with a plastic token in my hand before a range ball machine. I stood near the course, Hartfeld National, on a day filled with 50 professional people taking golf lessons in a dignified manner and matched outfits not ten feet away. The instructor's quiet voice sounded like a TV commentator's—barely above a whisper. It ran through my mind that some of those folks must surely have a hard time hearing this guy, or had taken a prerequisite course on lip reading.

I turned again to the machine. The instructions "Insert Card, Press Here" glared in bold red letters. Simple enough. I pressed the button and out poured a bucket of range balls. Only one problem: I failed to place the bucket under the spout to catch the darn things! Automatically, I shoved my hands into place, but it was too late. Those golf balls hit the concrete slab like a hailstorm, and bounced and rolled for what seemed to be an eternity.

Yep, everyone turned and stared, the instructor registered disgust, and the bag boys rolled on the ground in hysterical laughter. I wanted to shrink into the cracks of the concrete, but I had to pick up my mess. I gathered in utter shame.

Oh mercy, I wish I could say that these are isolated events in my life, but that would be a lie. One thing's for sure—life doesn't get dull. But, hey, I'd like a little bit of a breather between such humiliating episodes.

Thunderstruck

Summer in the south brings with it sudden and unexpected storms. They can be violent for just a few minutes, and leave a trail of destruction in their path. One such storm hit my marigolds and roses last Tuesday.

The patio was damp from the several minutes of sprinkle. As the thunder rolled in the background, something strange happened to all plants with blooms. The buds of the roses and the blossoms of the golden marigolds seemed to be snapped from the stem and dropped to the concrete edging. The thunder rolled all right, but there is more to the story. Let me back up a day.

Monday was bright and clear when the 4 X 4 truck, loaded to the top of the camper carrier with kids and stuff, rolled into the driveway. They were distant members of our family on their proverbial "summer trip" to the west and stopped by for a few days to visit, since they were in the same state. The concept was okay; the reality was different. Two of the four children were under 7 years old, and one was 15 going on 25. The middle one became rather much of a blur, so I can't even comment on what sex the child was.

The four-year-old had the eyes of an angel and the disposition of a monster from a Greek myth. Now, I had an active set of youngsters, and thought I was ready for anything. Either times have changed, or *I* have. Other than eating for a continuous 48 hours, having three TV's blaring cartoons or music videos amid the catfights for the remote controls, the bathrooms in a constant state of use, and the living room floor becoming dangerous with microscopic toys, everything was normal.

The thunder struck on Tuesday afternoon. A.D., the angel-demon, went outside, much to everyone's pleasure. He had been gone about ten minutes when he reappeared and urged me to come out, there was something to see. Truly, something to see: The marigolds, roses, salvia, and zinnias I had planted in a rainstorm and pampered and sprayed all summer had been deflowered by a different pest.

In a voice as sweet at Tweetybird's and eyes that twinkled with mischief, he announced, "Look what the thunder did!"

My mouth dropped open like the door of a mailbox. "Hey, I don't think the thunder could have done this, do you?" I struggled to remember that this was not my child, and the harmony of the family depended on me being diplomatic. "You don't really expect me to believe that thunder could be so dangerous?"

A.D. nodded and cut those clear blue eyes up at me in a challenging way.

I took his hand and spoke in my mother voice, "If the thunder does this again, lightning may strike close behind." The "D" didn't stand for "dummy," and I felt as if this bridge had been crossed, but I worried about the new bridges little A.D. would create before he got in the truck to go to the Wild West.

Wednesday was a beautiful day. I helped the gang pack up and begged them not to linger to help strip the beds and wash dishes. I even got great pleasure in strapping the seat belt on the little munchkins.

Yes, the sun shone brilliantly on the back window of the truck as they journeyed onward. The storm had hit. My house and my nerves were in shambles, but there is always such peace after a storm has been through, and I intended to savor it. Besides, the coffee was still on. As I raised my mug high in the air, I shouted with glee, "Go west, young man, go west!"

Puzzle

Friends of mine got me hooked on doing the daily crossword puzzle. I—the woman who won't play bridge or learn poker—have been tricked into worrying about four down and 26 across. It's so bad Sis has refused to walk through the kitchen unless on her way out the door, and Hon is ready to throw my dictionary away.

"Did you turn the coffee maker on?" Hon shuffles through the kitchen loving the lazy sunshine of summer.

"Huh? Coffee? I've got mine right here." I sink a bit deeper into the paper.

"Are we doing our own thing for breakfast, or are we going to have pleasant conversation and cholesterol this morning?"

"Huh? What is a six-letter word beginning with..."

"Great, you've found the puzzle already. I was hoping to get to the mailbox and tear out that section before you found it!" Hon pours his own coffee and pushes down the lever on the toaster. "Please pass the jelly."

"Can you tell me who the president of Brazil was in 1975? It will fill fifteen down. It begins with..."

Hon sits down and jerks the paper from my hands. "Hey, I know four and eighteen." He jots in the letters and spreads butter on his toast. "I think Aries is the god of war and Fairbanks is number nine down." He's hooked, and I forfeit my pencil to him until he is stuck and we both have to delve into the thesaurus.

As the time passes, I write my mom and pay all of the bills for the first of the month while he mumbles words and counts spaces to himself.

"Sweetheart, do you know the center of India's conservative political party in 1954? It could fill in the blank...." I don't have a clue who makes up these puzzles, but they should be staked over a bed of fire ants in the midday sun without help or water. Hon throws down the section of the paper with the puzzle only two-thirds finished. He reaches for the phone book.

"Who are you calling this early in the morning?"

"I'm calling my roommate from college. Only he would know what the record for catapulting over stone walls in the thirteenth century would be. That would answer forty-four across." He punches in the numbers.

"Hon, he's in California and several hours behind us. He's still in bed!"

"That's okay, he has woke me before for a lot less reason."

"Well, don't blame me if his answer is two letters shy of the blanks." Pouring coffee and spreading blackberry jam on my muffin is a tactic to keep me busy until I can get the page back into my own hands. It's a fun bridge we cross with mild perplexities and the phone numbers of friends who struggle through the same. By the way, do you know the goddess of love beginning with "A" and having...

Survival Of The Fittest

I have so many friends who are helpful to me, sometimes I feel I must reciprocate. With such generous intentions in the forefront of my mind, and with no grip on reality, I, the only woman in the neighborhood with a black thumb and cursed by the plant gods, offered to baby-sit two enormous Boston ferns. These plants were the proud result of a dear friend's long hours of diligent work and tender loving care. Why she asked, or why I agreed, I'll never understand unless I ask the TV psychics, for it has brought on worry lines and extra gray hairs.

"What if these things die?" I moaned aloud to Sis as I stared at the innocent plants. "The only thing I've managed to keep green for very long at a time is the mold in the refrigerator, or the lining of the shower curtain. And the time I tried to change my hair color and then go swimming. Boy, now that was a weird shade of green."

"Mom, you act like these plants have been left on your doorstep and you have a moral obligation to keep them alive. Cheer up! If they die, just buy her two more to replace these."

"You don't understand. It's like she's depending on me to help her out by tending to her babies. I promised to do everything I could to hand them over to her in better shape than they are now."

"You know something, Mom? You can get yourself into more situations. Tell you what—I'll water them and we'll let you-know-who talk to them. They say plants do better if you talk or sing to them."

"Well, then these beauties will be the size of Boston trees if Son talks to them, or else they'll just die in defense. Maybe Hon could hum them a

Scottish lullaby. Better yet, I could spray them green if they start to look sick. And there might be a plant hospital."

"Yeah! I never laughed so hard in my whole life as the time we watched that thirty-dollar plant you bought drop its leaves and petals as fast as if we were watching time-lapse photography. It did regroup though, didn't it? You have to admit, the best-looking plants in the house are the ones bought at Silk World. But I don't understand why you got this job. Did she see the plants in the living room?"

I shook my head and began mourning. "No, and she didn't see the wilting remnants of the violets in the kitchen window either. Now I've got to be positive. These two healthy globs are going to be just gorgeous when their mommie returns from her trip."

"Okay, but you better be looking for a bridge to a florist shop if they don't."

"I hear. I just hope those cute little fronds sitting over there by the air conditioner vents hear. Sis, did those things just nod at me?"

"Mom, it's been a long week. You need a rest. Remember the old saying, 'the fittest will survive'?"

"That's what worries me."

Necessities Of Packing

"You expect me to be gone for three weeks and pack only one suit-case? You've gotta be kidding. I pack two suitcases to go see my mother for three days!"

"I know that, but I can't carry four suitcases by myself. Those things weigh more than most *people*."

I could easily envision Hon looking like the bellhop for the Ritz-Carlton in New York, so I agreed to try to condense my daily requirements down to a reasonable traveling size. "Okay, but I don't think you have a grasp of my needs."

"Oh, yes I do. You need a full-time servant with the strength of a pro-fessional weight-lifter to manhandle your luggage, and I don't fit the job description."

Dismally, I retreated to the closet and my one open suitcase. "My new dress has got to go. And, this shirt will go with two things. If I color co-ordinate my wardrobe like they always tell you to do on those travel shows, I might can squeeze everything in." I pull out and hold up combination after combination. "It might rain, so I need a slick. It's very possible it will be chilly. That means I need to put in a sweater, socks, and take a jacket. High heels, low heels, scuffs, and sneakers." I tossed everything toward the open bag. The pile grew; time passed.

Hon peeked around the corner. "Are we going to eat tonight?"

"No, I thought we'd fast. That way I could wear two sets of clothes at the same time and not have to pack them." The look on Hon's face leads me to believe that he took me seriously, so I retracted the comment. "Of course we'll eat, dear. Why don't you whip up one of your special dinners while I conquer the rest of this job. I knew this would do one of two things: I'd get spaghetti, or go out to eat.

"We'll go get a hamburger in a little while." Then he spied the mountain of clothes and shoes. "Wait a minute. Do you plan to take all of this stuff?" His voice changed pitch three times before he finished the question. "Unless you are David Copperfield, you'll never get a third of that in one suitcase."

"Yes, I will. I have the biggest suitcase made. It's called the 'overseas case' and it holds a whopping amount." I began to fold and stack, and worry that his prediction would come true. "Give me one more hour and I'll be through this bridge with room to spare."

"If I were a betting man, I'd take you on, but I'll just go finish my own packing. I think I'll have half a suitcase empty if you need a little space." Hon grinned and hummed a little tune as he disappeared.

I would have a half a suitcase if all I needed was one change of underwear and socks. He expects me to have the hairdryer, ibuprofen, Imodium, telephone and address books, film and extra batteries, binoculars, and a dozen other little items in my bag or in my purse." I continued to bunch and pile.

I give up tonight. Maybe it can't be done. Maybe I'll go with an empty suitcase and buy everything I need! And maybe I'll hang half of this stuff back in the closet in the morning.

Just Waitin' For The Camera

I've filled in all the forms and stuffed them into the mail in plenty of time for the July Give-Away of ten million dollars. You can bet that I carefully read the questions sent to whet my imagination about being a millionaire.

Many of the inquiries deal with obtaining attorneys and other helpful professionals to encircle me once I am catapulted to the ranks of the rich and famous. Out of four pages of official looking information and surveying, my absolute favorite request asked permission to film me as one of their contest representatives award me the check! What a silly question. Of course they can film me—and what a front-page tabloid story it would be!

I can envision it now: Just out of the shower, my hair would have to be all dripping and ratty. My trusty five-year-old blue striped housecoat with its badges of household warfare would drape my matronly body. Don't even doubt that my favorite coffee mug with Shakespeare's caricature laughing at modern man would be in my right hand. As always is the case, if the doorbell rings, the phone rings a second later, so the portable phone with its call waiting feature going crazy would rest on my left shoulder. I haven't had the time to don the infamous pink fuzzy slippers. I go barefoot. It takes years of training and adaptation to do four tasks at one time.

Ah, yes. As the bell chimes, I swing the door open. I pray it is not one of several regulars: A cute gal dropping by to see Son (it always makes me feel like a slug when a twenty-year-old, all fresh and pencil thin, gives me the once over), the UPS man (who looks like Gene Wilder and thinks I'm insane to order aquatic plants from Texas), or my exterminator (who could blackmail me with his observations of my closets and/or my lack of house-keeping skills).

Oh, no! I open the door to a bouquet of balloons and flowers, a six-foot check, microphones, and cameras. Without the aid of my anti-wrinkle cream and moisturizing foundation, the cameras click and reporters shout all sorts of absurd questions.

"What's that you say? I've won ten million dollars?" Laughing and turning to Hon in disbelief, I would loudly ask, "Is this your idea of a joke, or is it Candid Camera? Either way, you may be in trouble for inventing this bridge for me to cross!"

No doubt, Ed McMahon would see me on a really bad hair day, but hey, for that kind of money I could get over it. Or better yet, stop the mailing campaign and save the rain forest.

Throwing In The Towel

"You know, brides sure have it lucky. They get all this new kitchen stuff that matches in design and color schemes. It's not like *our* stuff, Mom. This dishtowel I'm using is one of those calendars with the date, and this thing is from 1972! That's before I was born!" Sis seemed truly amazed that life existed in the house before either Son or she bounced onto the scene. She was rather bothered at the hodgepodge and abused condition of the items in our kitchen.

I must admit that, as I picked up the drying cloth from her hand, I had flashbacks of that year. "Yes, I always did like those cardinals on this cloth. Too bad there's a hole right next to the wing of the bright red one perched on the pine limb. Boy, the snow on the trees really cooled me off when I used this to wipe up all the mess of canning green beans and tomatoes in steamy July."

"Have you kept every one you got since you started housekeeping?"

"Watch your tone, young lady. No, I haven't, but these towels hold up forever and the older they are, the better they are to use. They're kinda like me. They have gotten soft with age."

"Brother! Nostalgia City. That means in our dishcloth drawer there are twenty more of these things? If you are comparing yourself to dishcloths, does that mean that you've also multiplied?"

I let Sis's comment pass on by without retaliation, for my curiosity got the better of me. How many had I kept out of the decades of housekeeping. The calendar cloths stuffed the drawer. "Maybe we'll just see how many I have. My mom used to give me a replacement calendar every year at Christmas. It was sort of a game to see how she would disguise it in the wrapping." I plundered through the drawer and found everything from birds and wildflowers, to cotton blooms, airplanes, and covered bridges.

"Why don't we put all these dishrags in a bag and get some new ones that match?" asked Sis.

"What's wrong with these? We have plenty and the holes don't bother me. Here's one from the bicentennial year with a revolutionary soldier in red, white, and blue. Here's another you might be interested in looking at more closely." I tossed her the ragged one with Hollie Hobby in her blue and white pioneer dress waving a flag imprinted with 1976 and 13 little stars. "That's a memento of the year you were born."

Suddenly, Sis began to enjoy the trip through this bridge as I retold a story of 1978's calendar and the family events of that year. Children always enjoy hearing stories about the way they were as babies. I should tell them more, so that the oral history of their lives and those of their network of family isn't lost.

"Where's 1993 and 1994?"

"Oh, I stopped getting dishcloths several years back. Guess Mom thought I had an ample supply and it sorta lost vogue. You know, it's rather like missing a copy of *National Geographic*."

"Mom, get real. This one with the daisies is cute."

"Yeah, those were the colors of my kitchen when I was a young house-wife. Green and gold aren't quite as popular today."

"But, just think. The sixties pop art is returning. Some of these dish-towels will come back into fashion."

"Uh huh. About the time you get the dishes dried. Give me the one with the covered bridge on it and I'll help you out. We'll cross this bridge with smiles on our faces and memories in our hearts."

Plumbing

Travel can be stimulating and educational. Case in point: On our last jaunt away from the Gulf, Hon and I stayed with relatives, in hotels, and at a few Bed and Breakfasts. In our entire trip and with all of our accommodations, the biggest challenge turned out to be not the drive or timing, but the bathrooms and plumbing. I'm here to witness to you that there are no two faucets alike in the eastern part of the United States. Either the fixtures date back to the turn of the century, or are so ultra-modern only a rocket scientist can walk in and work them the first time.

A Bed and Breakfast can be charming, and the ambiance can send me into another time and place, but if I scald myself with the hot water from the shower, "dressing for dinner" takes on new meaning. Another problem in many of the older houses is that clogged pipes and septic systems can bring about disgruntled anxiety. The stream of water often dribbles out of the showerhead—no joy to a sweaty traveler. The drainage problems accompanying one stay made me fear the lip of the stall wouldn't be deep enough to hold all my sudsy water, so I hurried through. One place did have an antique footed tub like I remember my grandmother had in her house out in the country. It could float a battleship, and I needed a life preserver and ladder, but it was a fine bath. I took my snorkel in with me and soaked for an hour.

Hotel chains and newer lodgings flaunt state of the art fixtures. That's great, but in Bristol, Virginia, after a six-hour drive and a three-hour walk to see the Natural Bridge in 96-degree heat and humidity, all I wanted was a bath and to prop my feet up in front of the TV. It took me 30 minutes to push, pull, twist, and adjust the knobs on the shower. By that time, my exhaustion grew into frustration and even a mindless movie didn't put me in a better humor.

Now let's address the habitats of dear relatives. True, I can't legitimately gripe about free lodging, but some of my clan's bathrooms rate in the top ten for torture chambers. A cousin, in the throes of remodeling, didn't have her air conditioner installed properly; therefore, taking a shower became a moot point. My brother's new bathroom had ill-fitting shower curtains, and all of the clothes I brought in to wear got soaked. Mom's place—well, in truth, the most pressure at her house is limiting the calorie count at the dinner table so as to still fit into her bathroom. The list could go on.

I felt happiest when I hopped into my own shower stall last Monday night. I was home from all the adventures, and ecstatic to realize that it would not be a new learning experience to work all the fixtures. I jumped in, grabbed the shampoo, and began an aria from *Carmen*. The water ran steaming hot, then icy cold, the pressure went from blockbusting to a drizzle. What? In *my* shower? I crawled into bed mumbling something about communist plots.

Although I have met each challenge with an undaunted heart, I wonder if this bridge has an end at all.

ATM's

"Twenty-seven million transactions are made at ATM machines every day in America. No wonder I can't get cash out of the darn things! Millions of people have beaten me to it." With disgust, Son planted the little informational flyer from the bank down on the kitchen counter I was cleaning, and grabbed a soda.

"No, the reason you can't get money out of the machine is that there is no money in the account," I quipped.

Son shrugged his shoulders, then bantered, "Well, at least I can remember my PIN number and follow the directions on the screen. I'd love a copy of the videotape from the surveillance camera when you stood in front of the machine downtown and tried to get cash. I'll bet the security team at the bank fell down in hysterics."

"It wasn't that funny. Just because I ran the card through backwards a couple of times isn't cause for laughter." I huffed and scrubbed the sink.

"No, but when you started talking to the camera like there was a real person in the back, it brought tears to my eyes." Son lifted his hands in defense, "But hey, I'm glad no one was around to see you put your hands on your hips and explain the reason you needed the money to a blinking screen. And even though *you* didn't think so, the directions were in English." Son continued his litany of the incident without even pausing for air. "Then you kept looking around like you were some sorta criminal. It's a wonder the police didn't drive by and nab you." Son stopped long enough to gulp the soda and enjoy the moment.

I squirted cleaner and swiped at the counter with my dishcloth, then replied, "Well, I've heard all these tips on how to be safe around ATM's. A newscaster did a TV segment on personal security. He said to look around and be aware of the surrounding environment. And I decided to hide my PIN number behind my coupons for antacids so no one can find it."

"Yeah, but you looked like the gal in the movie *Bonnie & Clyde*."

"Humph. That's impossible. She weighed all of ninety-eight pounds soaking wet and was a real mean killer."

"OOPS! Sorry, Mom. Maybe you looked like Bonnie and Clyde together. And you've killed enough houseplants to be listed in *Ripley's Believe It or Not*." He dodged the expected glare by ducking into the refrigerator.

"I'll get the hang of those contraptions yet. They're supposed to be a convenience, not a major stress factor in my life. And, say what you will, I did finally get the money I wanted."

Son hugged and soothed me. "You didn't even thank me when I got out of the car and punched in all the information. Mom, I know that, by the time you learn to work those machines, there will be colonies on Mars."

"Well good," I responded. "The flyer also said that the U.S. Postal Service handles 495 million pieces of mail a day. Maybe they'll launch a branch office there so I can get deliveries."

Catalog Queen

"According to the U.S. Bureau of the Census, $325 million a day was spent on mail order sales of consumer products and services," said Hon, putting down the business and financial section of his paper. "And I think every one of those businesses sent you a catalog with a toll-free number on the cover."

"I like my catalogs, thank you. There's stuff in them you can't find anywhere else," I replied in a defiant tone, and poked my head into a section of the paper to read the garden tips.

"You know, the Postal Service handles 495 million pieces of mail a day. About 367 million of those pieces must come to our box addressed to Occupant, a term you find endearing; Resident, a name which seems to give you confidence; or..."

He was about to continue when I cut in: "Yes, but I like the extra note printed on the envelopes which warn the postal person not to forward this to any other address. That way, I know I'll get what's coming to me!"

"But do we need a brochure of campers and RV's? We don't own one." His query rang true, and he pushed forward: "And how about the bathing suit sale ad that came yesterday. If you find enough cloth on all the suits in the thirty-page catalog to make one suit for you, I'll take you to the Riviera."

Suddenly, he had crossed the line—insulted my pride and stirred my curiosity. "How'd you know there were 30 pages in the book?"

"I flipped through it before I trashed it." He felt the explanation enough.

"Oh, well then. I can toss that red and white catalog with the airplane parts on the front."

"Hey, don't do that. Those parts are hard to find and it has lots of phone numbers and a price list. It'll save money when I have gizmos to replace."

"*Your* catalogs are okay, but mine are endangering the Rain Forest. I get the full glossy picture."

"Look, if you want me to save all we get from week to week, I'll have to build another room onto the house." Defensively, Hon snapped the pages of the paper as he held them high to turn the pages and fold.

"I know I get a lot of junk catalogs, but sometimes I get great ideas. Remember that Christmas present I ordered for Auntie?"

"You mean the nose hair clippers?" Hon ducked low into his pages and cackled.

"Very funny. No-o-o, I mean those slippers with the built-in foot warmers. Those were nice."

"Yep. I just hope there is a disclaimer stating that we can't be sued if she gets electrocuted. Look, sweetheart, I won't hassle you any more about all this if you will just promise me that you'll throw out at least half and only order from one a week from the rest." My stubborn silence ended the conversation. But a few days later, Hon bridged it to a new discussion as he strolled into the den with a paper crown and pompously pronounced, "Here, I crown you not only Queen of the House, but also the Catalog Queen of the South."

I stared up from the Garden Lovers Spring sale book and planted a kiss on his cheek while simultaneously pointing to a picture in the catalog. "Thanks, but do you think I could order this wheelbarrow to haul all my stuff?"

"I suppose." There was a dramatic pause as he flipped through the stack of mail, then sat down to the e-mail. He exploded, "I can't believe it. You've got catalogs through e-mail, too!"

I smiled, deserving of my new title, and adjusted my crown.

Fall Bridges

Through the bridges of fall we return to routine. Once again, the children sit in classrooms, and schedules fill up with meetings and game times. It's a busy, busy time; we don't want to miss a thing, even though survival is sometimes questionable.

Labor Day

One of the true holidays of the year is Labor Day. No one expects a present, nor is there any rush to the beach to get a tan. Instead, my family just fires up the grill one more time and grabs the nearest shade and lawn chair to soak up this, the last long sigh of summer.

Traditionally, my maternal side of the family spends the day at a river house owned by an aunt. The variety of ages and activities mirrors the diversity of our growing group. Cousins who used to be ugly teenagers are now taxpaying family folk, and my own two children have reached the age of "do I have to go?"

Son exclaims that the first sentence anyone over 30 utters is an observation on how much he has grown, only to be punctuated by scented hugs and kisses. "But these are your roots, Son, your human heritage. I have to allow them to kiss you and bless you just as if they were giving the papal blessings." He will slink back to his room to get a headphone to offset any conversation he wishes to ignore.

Sis will bounce out of her room in the latest denim wear and flaunt the glow of the ankle bracelets purchased on vacation. She won't verbalize her unhappiness. In my mind, I can quote Grandmother's remarks verbatim the moment she spies any outfit even remotely stylish. I hope nothing is ever mentioned about Nehru jackets or the white go-go boots and mini-skirts of my generation.

After the initial shock of all the haircuts and hair losses, the paper plate lunch on Labor Day is glorious. The spread is topped with several varieties of homemade ice cream. And then we all languidly watch children play in the grass or fish from the pier. Discussions of the good and the bad, the past and the future, seem appropriate. It sits at our side or plays at our feet at that very moment.

The dogwood trees that line the driveway turn a brilliant crimson by the first weekend in September. And as the waning afternoon nudges us to depart, we realize the next holidays we spend together will not be so relaxed and comfortable. We are traveling through a bridge leading into a busy fall.

Sounds Of Fall

"Man, I just love Saturdays in the fall." Son poured milk over his cornflakes and grabbed the remote control.

I squinted at the clock above the pantry. "It's only 8:30 in the morning. Are you sick? Did you just *not* go to bed last night?"

"Mom! Are you kidding? This is one of the biggest football weekends until bowl season!" Son gave me the I-can't-believe-you-mean-that stare.

"Well, just call me dumb, but what has that got to do with it being 8:30? Besides, you're speaking in riddles."

"The first pre-game show starts in just a few minutes."

"But it's 8:30 in the morning, not 8:30 at night. I'm baffled. Where are they playing? England?"

"No, Dublin."

"Excuse me, my hearing aid must have been disconnected."

Son proceeded into the den and said, "Let me see.... There." He punched on the den TV. "Technology is a wonderful thing." Suddenly, the room vibrated, the windows rattled, and the crystal glasses in the china cabinet tinkled against one another as he switched on the new speakers adjacent the large screen. "Surround sound makes me feel almost like I'm in the stadium. All I need is a three-dollar hotdog and a bag of peanuts. Listen to the roar of that crowd." Genuine excitement filled his voice.

"Yeah, well if you throw peanut hulls on my new carpet, all the emergency numbers in the book won't help you."

He disregarded my comment. "Boy, this PIP is great! Look, I can put another game in this corner and switch back and forth between three or four games and never see a commercial."

"I thought we bought a set with the PIP to keep up with the weather channel."

"Mom, did you really believe that line?"

"Well, now that you come to mention it...."

"My buddy at school has the new satellite system. He gets over a hundred channels, twenty-four hour sports, and pay-for-view boxing." The excitement had not faded.

"The day I pay to see someone beat up and bloody the nose of another guy I'll turn in my apron. Anyhow, you can't possibly absorb more than one or two games at a time."

"That's a typical mother response. You *tape* them!"

I gave my head a V-8 slap. "Golly, why didn't I think of that. If you lived to be two hundred thirty-six you'd never...I need some coffee." I left him there reassured that he would be there until he ran out of food. "Eight-thirty on Saturday mornings in the fall should be for wandering through country bridges and old shops, not spanning the globe for ticketed altercations.

Hon walked through the kitchen with a mug in one hand and his glasses in another. "Hey, where's the remote control? Today's a big football..."

I pointed toward the den. "I'm going to grab the camera and take pictures of bridges and go shopping."

He never gave me a glance as he plunked down on the den couch.

Getting The Blues

Some things in life should be simple and basic. Buying a pair of blue jeans should be one of them. I have purchased jeans for my kids and me without too much trauma, but I have yet to recover from my latest experience just this week.

As I stood in the front door of the large specialty store and gazed at four walls filled ceiling to floor with neatly folded denim, I developed a false sense of security. Even the hundred or so racks around the room burgeoned with nothing but jeans. I surely had come to the right place.

A sales clerk, younger than my children, zipped up to me and asked if she could help. I must have appeared a bit matronly as I blurted out Hon's size and length.

"Does he want relaxed fit or regular?"

"What does that mean?"

She explained, and I supplied her with some kind of muddled reply.

"Straight legged or tapered?"

I couldn't answer that as easily.

"Stone washed, faded...."

"I just want plain ole denim!" The beginning of a tension headache throbbed. The next thing she would ask would be my preference of smoking or non-smoking.

With her rehearsed "the customer is always right" attitude, the clerk backed away and stood waiting for me to give her an answer so that the process could continue. She was treating me like a pre-schooler having a temper tantrum. My blood pressure went up even more.

"I tell you what. How about finding me a pair that is a standard color and big enough to be comfortable even if my husband continues to eat regularly. Elastic in the waist would be great." The last statement was intended to be a tease, but the gal took me seriously and puzzled for a moment.

"I think we have a few pair on the far wall with elastic..."

I raised my hand and stopped her mid-sentence. "Forget the elastic and let's just find his size. Okay?" She marched me to the right wall. I wondered if a firing squad might appear from behind door number two if I answered in an insubordinate vein again. Interrogations from the FBI couldn't be more detailed. The child/clerk had stopped walking and scanned the labeled shelves for the size I had given her. "Lady, this may be a little difficult. We don't stock too many jeans in this length."

This remark was the last straw. "What does that mean?"

She was roving again like a reporter taking a poll. Ten minutes later and completely across the store, the clerk dug into a pile and surfaced with a pair of white jeans the size and length I needed. She awarded them to me with the pride of an an investigator uncovering a case-breaking clue.

"These are *white*!" This initial excitement skyrocketed as I considered the price tag. "Forty-eight dollars! I don't pay this kind of money for a Sunday dress, much less jeans. You're supposed to get dirty and sweaty in jeans, or sit on hay, or take your kids to the park in them. These are white. Hon couldn't even manage to put them on without getting them dirty. I'll have to try every new bleach on the market."

I could see Hon's face when I tossed him this prize. I would never live it down, but I didn't hand them back to her. This bridge had taken too long to cross. "Okay, I'll take 'em." Was this my voice? I must be having an out-of-body experience.

The girl nodded, then lifted her chin and bravely asked, "Now what about your pair?"

My current predicament was proving much too punishing to my ego, and besides, I'd have to float a loan to get several pair. "I think I'll see if these fit and come back for mine," I lied. I really intended to see if Son or Sis had any discards we could wear.

I left the store singing the blues. Also, with a resolution to hire a member of the younger generation to shop for my jeans.

Buying School Supplies

Aware that the beginning of school would require a shopping trip for supplies, I laced up my most comfortable sneakers and prepared for the worst.

Unlike my mom, who could dash to the five-and-ten and purchase a pack of loose-leaf paper and a blue three-ringed binder for each of her children, I knew today's chore would be challenging and the lines long. The current school supply market is specialized and high-fashioned. A person would have to have slept for ten years not to know that fact. I would not be a happy or relaxed person by supper tonight.

While Sis informed me she had only an hour to spare before her next round of phone appointments began, I retrieved Son from the 24-hour video game he plays. Not much later, we all stood reluctantly in the store aisle gazing at the unbelievable stacks of pens, papers, and paraphernalia. Our annual ritual began. We were not alone.

Twenty-five sets of parents and offspring just like us grabbed for the latest Trappers.

One child wanted lavender college ruled paper; the other required perforated edges in a neon striped cover. I wistfully re-shelved a Nifty blue binder when Son squawked that it was "generic" and Sis rolled her blue eyes in disbelief. And black and blue ballpoint pens are as endangered as some species of animals in Africa. We tossed electric-pink, pea-green, fine-point, and fat markers into the cart.

Finally, I called time on all this family fun and maneuvered my way to the check-out line. Great—I was only backed up halfway to the household detergents. It took an hour to reach the cashier, during which time both children milked me for extra arcade money, cokes, and quarters to use in the pay phone.

By the time I reached the top of the line, I had daydreamed my way back through the bridge where there were only yellow pencils and white paper. The question, "Would that be cash or charge?" brought me quickly back.

List And Tales

"Mom, I need a refrigerator for my room." Sis eyed me squarely and added, "and an answering machine for our portable phone. My roommate is going to bring the VCR and TV, so I'll need to get the microwave as well."

I shook my head to clear my ears. Could I really be hearing these requests from my college-bound daughter? This little girl that I've loved and cradled in my arms? The one that's an expert in internet and mashing buttons, but hasn't a clue of how to start the dishwater. "Excuse me, did you say microwave?"

She nodded with an air of affirmation.

I knew in my parental heart of hearts it was time—time to drag out and explain in complete detail my "ten-miles-uphill-both-ways-in-the-snow-to-school" stories. My folks did it to me and I grew up pretty normal, so now my kids can tough it out. Besides it's rather fulfilling to recount chosen ones with enough embellishment to make a lover of Italian rococo sick.

"You know, Sis, I lived on a dollar a week from my parents. My Dad would lose the rest of his hair if I told him you needed this list of stuff. It sounds like you're setting up housekeeping, not getting ready for class."

"Yes, Mom, you've told me the story a hundred times. Let me see...you had a meal ticket and a roof over your head, so he didn't feel you needed anything else. And, of course, the university allowed only seniors to have a car on campus."

"That was easy to live with. I didn't own a car until I graduated, married, and had a job." I nodded the way old folks do when affirming the gospel in a tent meeting. "Did I ever tell you that freshmen girls had to sign in and out of the dorm, and that our curfew was ten o'clock?"

Sis cackled. "All of these rules and regulations in the Age of Bra Burnings and Civil Rights. Are you sure you aren't telling someone else's story?"

My eyes darted instantly her way. "We walked to classes and into town—in heat and cold—yeah, even in rain and snow." I quickly phased onto memory lane. "One of the best times we ever had was the week in January when classes were canceled because of snow. We seized the plastic trays from the cafeteria and used them to sled down the hills. The campus nurse lived in our dorm, and let me tell you, some of the cutest boys got hurt and had to be carried into our hallway. It gave new meaning to the shout, 'Man on the hall!'"

"Mom! Get back into reality. Would you also put on our shopping list tract-feed paper. It's easier to use in my computer printer."

"What ever happened to shopping for pencils and notebooks? Did they close that bridge down, or have I just taken a detour?"

"Not sure, Mom. By the way, have you checked my e-mail today?"

My shoulders sagged for a moment. Then I raised my index finger. "Did I ever tell you about...."

A Biting Tale

Fall and football have always been synonymous occurrences in our house, and as I hear the familiar clash and roar of the games on TV, I am personally reminded of my major clash with a budding football star just a few seasons ago.

It was in the early fall of 1991, and Son was an aspiring high school guard on the local team. Crusty shoes with cleats adorned my entrance hall; shirts and pants caked with mud draped my washer and dryer. Son proudly wore a lingering and unpleasant odor of locker room. As a mom, I always tried to support his ambitions, but there are some things team spirit and enthusiasm just won't conquer. That also applies to a rookie mom's knowledge of the routine care of personal equipment.

"You know we go out in pads tomorrow, so I've got to boil my new mouthpiece before I go to bed tonight." Son's voice had all the excitement of a player under a multi-million dollar contract.

I could have had a few choice comebacks to that statement. For example, "Maybe you could wear it when you're at home," or "If you can boil a mouthpiece, why can't you microwave your supper?" I let this royal opportunity pass with silence, but the conversation in my brain continued. "I'll just wait to see if you actually do something ahead of schedule, or if you'll be pleading with me to bring it to you after school."

The afternoon passed, dinner passed, and bedtime passed. The mouthpiece lay in its plastic ziplock bag by the stove awaiting its fate and, like a true player in a Greek tragedy, would meet its undoing at sunrise.

It was a gorgeous autumn morning and I had gotten enough sleep (something rare). As I made my coffee, I caught a glimpse of the unstarted project from the night before. "Hum," I said to myself, "Son said he needed his mouthpiece boiled, so to keep panic from ensuing in 45 minutes, I'll just do it for him. I used to boil bottles and the like when he was a baby. This can't be any different." Now, keep in mind that I had had plenty of sleep, and God always knows when you are going to need plenty of sleep. The pot of water boiled with vigor as I snipped the end of the bag. Without reading the instructions, I tossed the odd-shaped thing into the tempest and went about my morning chores.

A while later, I wandered back to the stove and leaned over to check the progress. "Oh, dear, what has happened?" I moaned. "I don't think Son can use this." Sure enough he couldn't. The U-shaped mouthpiece with its knotty tail now floated atop the boiling water, a gnarled wad of plastic with no shape at all! I swooped out the mangled stuff. "This isn't going to be easy to explain," I mumbled as I walked solemnly to Son's room.

The stoic announcement of the ruin was met with wild bellowings. The ancient Greek chorus would have been proud of this show of grief. Son bounded to the stove only to wail more. But as the phoenix of mythology rose from its ashes, so rose the mouthpiece. Placing the pliable plastic back into the boil then into his mouth, Son mashed and chomped and spit it out with a rather recognizable impression of his teeth. "I'll have to cut this weird looking tail off. It was supposed to go around my face mask, but this will have to do. I'll be the only lineman in the world with a bobtailed mouthpiece. Guess you're gonna have to explain this one to the coach yourself, Mom." Son's voice had adult determination in it as he stared at the plastic lump in his hand.

I stood there a moment, shamed by the fact I had not read the directions and pitying myself for having made such a noble effort only to fail at the task.

But hey, this bridge taught me a memorable lesson in motherhood: Let children do for themselves before you do it to them!

Sacked

With the onset of field-trip and picnic season comes the fun of packing sack lunches and snacks. Ever since the children were big enough to need a portable lunch, I've decorated the outside of the bag with crayon drawings of the anticipated event (animals for the zoo, clowns for the circus, space ships for the rocket center). My child's name would appear in colorful, easy-to-spot letters. It started as a surprise for Son, but turned into an expected tradition.

The last time I packed Sis off to a field trip on a museum, I thought she was past the age of wanting to have stick people and balloons on her bag, but I was wrong. She returned home a very disappointed girl. "Mom, you have always decorated my lunch sack. Why didn't you do it this time? I expected to find little picture frames or statues on my brown paper."

"I'll do better next time, sweetheart." I decided against using the excuse of not having enough time to decorate a sack for fear she would retaliate with one of my own comments: You always have time to do the things you really want to do. Shamed, I resolved to be sure not to let it happen again, and opportunity did not wait long to knock.

Son had an outing planned and needed a lunch and canned drink to tide him over until real food could be devoured. I grabbed my crayons and went to work. I put his name in bold letters and embellished the sides with footballs and school symbols. After filling the insides with sandwiches and cookies, I went about my business.

It was not until afternoon that I got any sort of feedback on the artistry. "Mom, you must know ten thousand ways of embarrassing me."

"What have I done now?" I didn't raise my eyes or voice; there was no need. I would be informed in a matter of seconds.

"I'm not in the first grade anymore and I don't need my name on my lunch. Everybody knew whose bag it was, so they helped themselves to the cookies and I had to give away my cheese crackers to the birds because they weren't crackers anymore, just crumbs."

"Well, how are you supposed to know which meal is yours if names aren't on them?"

"Mom, it's fun to see what everybody has and swap up. I traded my apple for a candy bar. There was one advantage though. The girls thought my lunch sack was cute, but I don't think that will offset the kidding I'm gonna get from the guys. They'll sack me like the quarterback of some bad NFL team and I'll never know what hit me!"

Moms never get it right. The bridges we cross are often long tunnels of confusion, and just about the time we think we have an understanding of what's going on, a new turn in the situation appears and our directions are altered once more. I haven't made up my mind what I'll do when the next outing comes along, but the crayons won't be very far away.

In The Sun

It is the last of September; therefore, I am wearing my tenth pair of sunglasses of the season. It doesn't seem to matter what kind, what color, or price—I manage to mangle more pair than a defensive tackle for the 49'ers. Because of my destructive nature, I buy bargain glasses—you know, the three-for-a-dollar ones in the middle aisle of the discount store. Or I take advantage of the cereal box offers (I have two pair coming with Goofy on the sides).

Son has since given up riding or even walking with me when I am donning sunglasses. "Mom, you aren't going to wear those glasses that are on the kitchen counter, are you?"

"Well, yes, Son. Why do you ask?"

"They have pink elephants on them. People will think you're nutty. I'm not walking in to register for classes with you modeling those things!"

"Hey, every five-year-old in town will know where I got them. I had to eat four boxes of Tooty Frooty Loops to get enough UPC codes to send off for them. Then I had to wait four weeks for delivery. I went through two more pair of sunglasses before these arrived."

"Mom, you mean to tell me you meant to get those things and wear them? One thing's for sure, no one will steal them. Have you ever thought of wearing a nondescript pair of plain brown or black?"

"Sure, I even paid twenty dollars for a pair one time. After I spent twenty minutes scraping off the sticker, I put them in the seat of the car so I could wear them when driving on bright days. Guess what happened five minutes after that! Uh, huh. I got back to the car from buying groceries and threw my purse on the seat. When I picked up the purse, the glasses were history. They looked like they had been through the bombing of Pearl Harbor."

"Why don't you wear them on the top of your head like everyone else in the world?"

"Naw. That's too simple. I'd rather collect cereal box tops."

"I want a pair of those pilot glasses. They only cost a hundred and fifty."

"A hundred and fifty what? Surely you don't mean dollars. Why, for that amount of money I could buy an outfit in the latest fall color."

"It's all the rage on campus these days."

"Well it might be the rage, but I'll be in a rage if I find out you've spent that kind of money on sunglasses that you'll wear a few days at most. Lay them down and what do you think will happen?"

"I knew I would get this lecture. It's number five hundred six: you-don't-understand-the-value-or-take-care-of-things lecture. It can be delivered on paper, tape, and even over the phone."

"I'll eat four more boxes of cereal and get you some green ones just like these. I've gotten used to the taste."

"Of the cereal or the glasses? No thanks, I'll just wear the ones you have left from last year that have one side wired on with a bread tie."

Well, it seems I am stuck on this bridge of stylish need. I read where sunglasses were an outward symbol of our personality! I feel a certain sense of panic. In my purse are three pair, all with some deformity of lens or limb. "Lord, I hope it's not true. I can't be this warped."

"Mom, you are mumbling to yourself again. Don't sweat it. I'm not about to wear pink or green elephants, nor will I wear any of your menagerie of styles and colors. But you're right. They do give you character."

"Thanks. Maybe I should just squint and have lines around my eyes. Don't you think that would make me look distinguished? Don't even answer that one out loud."

"No, I think I'd better go with you as your keeper and trainer!"

Weather Channel

We've all logged enough hours on the weather channel to feel like we deserve a framed certificate in meteorology. Just give folks on the coast a tropical depression in Mexico and out come the tracking charts. And as Opal marched toward the panhandle, Hon began to put the weather channel on his remote control loop of stations—right there with the NFL Monday football and *Biography*.

"Looks like she could come our way," Hon announced with the tone of a southern evangelist, "but maybe she'll turn east and we can dodge the bullet one more time."

That was Monday night. Tuesday morning brought the deluge of rain and updated predictions of what might head our way. "I hope I can get to the grocery store and get some essentials before the lines back up to the meat counters."

"Mom, be sure to get something other than diet drinks. Get some real cookies and salsa. Get good stuff, please," Son whined as he opened the door for me.

"Broccoli is good for you, but I'll get a bag of high fat chips and ice cream as well. Okay? Happy?"

I listened to the radio as I returned home. The school closings and current storm coordinates grabbed my attention. Hope I have enough paper towels and plates to last, I thought to myself, especially if those winds stay at 150 miles per hour and head west.

Dumping the bags on the kitchen counter, I turned to watch the TV weatherman from Mobile give his most up-to-date predictions and compare Opal to Frederick and Camille. Things could get nasty. I hope I have enough batteries. The rains continued and Hon became an expert on latitude and longitude as he poked the pins onto corkboard chart defining an ever-northward trail.

Wednesday morning: A deja vu from Erin. Go to bed with a hurricane watch and wake up being in the strike zone and hearing continuous coverage on every channel about precautions and open shelters. I hope I have enough bread and cereal.

With my patio furniture stacked in my den, and my ferns practically begging to come in, I filled everything from pots to tubs with water to the drone of information coming from the tube.

"What would we use water in the tub for, Mom?" Sis quizzed as she filled the Igloo cooler.

"You don't ask questions like that at a time like this. It's like in the westerns when the doctor always tells the cowpoke assisting him to boil some water. You just do it." Strangely, the answer seemed to satisfy her.

In the background, the gal on TV rattled..."gather important papers...."

I began the search for insurance policies and all the "important papers" we scatter in drawers all over the house. "I'm too old to have to know where my birth certificate is, and the kids have had all of their shots. I hope I have enough Band-Aids in the first aid kit," I grumbled to the new announcer (Hon had flipped channels again).

By mid-afternoon, every family member hoping to be mentioned in our wills had called. "We were just watching the weather channel. I hope you have enough candles and ice. Did you tape up your windows?" Our uncle from the west coast queried like a schoolmarm.

By late afternoon, we slumped into chairs and played cards while the wind blew and the rain poured. By now, we knew every weather forecaster on the planet on a first-name basis. "I hope we have enough flashlights and radio batteries," someone said.

Seven o'clock. I knew we would be okay when the cable and color came back on and the commentator for the Braves called out the balls, strikes, and errors instead of a forecaster spouting out measurements of barometric pressure in millibars. It was with great relief that the household realized our bridges were safe and began to sympathize with those whose bridges were gone. We turned the set off. We'd had enough.

No Deposit, No Return

I have gained magnitudes of insight in the area of personal freedoms since my daughter reached the height and weight of a grown woman. Perhaps gain is the wrong term; loss would be more accurate. I found out nothing is off limits to her anymore—not jewelry, makeup, clothes, cologne—my list seems to multiply and become endless.

I have also established that the only time I don't have a keen sense of fashion is when standing at a half-priced rack in a downtown department store, but the shirt bought despite Sis's look of consternation is borrowed and worn with jeans in less than 48 hours. Mom's outfits also gain a new respect in the times when there is nothing else freshly laundered. I began to think that I should acquaint Sis with the bottle theory: No deposit, no return. But, I recollected that theory doesn't work as well in practice as it promises to on paper.

In the car a few mornings ago, I noticed my favorite pair of earrings dangling from earlobes other than my own. We didn't have time for too much discussion, so the conversation ended with a humoring, "I'll put them right back in the box this afternoon, I promise." Those words rang louder than the school bell and my heart sank low. I knew for a fact that if the earrings did indeed return to their original box, they would be the first items in recent history to do so.

It seems I have had a great deal of trouble keeping my stockings, good sweaters, bracelets, and the like from the all-grabbing hands. I really like to keep a nice pair of Sunday stockings. So does Sis. I like mine without holes. So does Sis. I never have a pair in the drawer. Yet, Sis always has a pair on her legs as she jumps into the car.

The last boundary was crossed just last Thursday. I hopped into the shower and prepared to lather up my legs, reached for the razor and cream, only to discover that they, too, had been borrowed. Betoweled and bewildered, I streaked through the house to retrieve my belongings, knowing that my own mom must be smiling somewhere at delayed justice.

And as I dripped down the hall, I suddenly realized that this was going to be a long, long bridge, and the crossing might never be completed, for I also remembered the brooch and earrings borrowed 20 years ago from my mom. They are in the top drawer of my dresser.

Computer II

Well, I'm on-line with the rest of America, and the information super highway, like the autobahn, does not have a speed limit. And as with any new area, the lingo to go along with it has changed the meaning of common words in my language.

Take, for example, the word "browser." To the average woman in middle-America, right here before all the holiday sales signs go up, the word should mean casually looking for gifts or sales stuff. I've been at the professional level of browsing since my high school days. On-line browsing is a lot more difficult to manage. Instead of leisurely strolling the aisles of my favorite mall, I sit at my monitor and bang on the keyboard in frustration. Pinpointing the information is at the minimum a three-hour task, and that means no one gets supper or their clothes washed. I'm irritable, Hon's unkempt, Sis can't talk on the phone, and Son is hungry. We aren't happy campers.

Then there is "surfing." Once upon a year ago, Son's idea would have been to hit the waves at the beach and enjoy the day. He hits internet surfing with the same happy-go-lucky attitude as a Beachboys event. Although not as intense as browsing, surfing can get tricky. We all ended up either flooded with more information than anyone would ever use, or washed out.

"User domain" has to be one of my favorite changes in terms. Hon always defined "domain" as his place in front of the TV and controlling the remote. Not today. Domains can be as far away as England and Italy (I can read Pope John Paul's latest speech, if only I could translate from Italian to English), or as close as the neighbor down the block.

"Menu," a popular concept with the entire family, can now bring on mumblings and expletives needing deleting. Okay, you still look at the listings and you still make choices—and hey, there are no calories. Menus may turn out to be okay, but then there are those world-wide web searchers.

The expressions given to these "creatures of the line" fit, I suppose, but "Gopher"? Please! I still remember the title defined as a person who, being lowest on the totem pole, has to fetch everything. Well, on second thought, maybe it is correctly identified. However, the "search engine," (don't you just love *that* term), I feel suits me best is the Webcrawler. Yep, most of the time I am on my hands and knees more than a medieval monk in my quest for information. And, in another light, I crawl like an infant through the maze of http's, url's, and ftp sites.

The most important feature on the computer with its on-line programs is the "home" button and escape. I can always turn the machine off, or choose to bolt across the bridge of high-tech inventions. But, I am master of the only mouse I want in my den, and doing Windows '95 on the computer is closer to the reality of getting it done by Son than if I hand him a Windex bottle. Sure, just like learning to program my microwave, I'll get the hang of this operation yet!

Approach To Cleaning

"D-Day is here. We are going to be forced to clean up the office store-room. The carpet guys can't possibly move all those boxes and books and put carpet down as well. They'll walk off the job." The affirmative tone of Hon's message signaled me not to try to question or to negotiate another postponement (I had already stalled three times).

"Fine, I'll go over later this afternoon."

"No, we are *both* going."

My heart sank low, for Hon and I attack cleaning from different points of view. He is a "thrower," and I am a "keeper." This cleaning adventure could stress even the most docile person to the point of needing medication.

When I moved three years ago from a house with a full basement (both literally and figuratively), I was forced to condense all my paraphernalia into boxes which could be put in the tiny office store room. I survived the paring and was actually proud of my efforts, and the storeroom proved to be a great place for all the family photo albums, baby books, and senti-mental memorabilia. The kids were exceptionally happy. With the embar-rassing photos several miles away, I couldn't show them to their friends and dates.

The task began easily enough. Throw away that stack of old maga-zines. Start a pile for a rummage sale. Then on to the serious weeding.

"What's all this stuff in here? Do you want this old picture of you and the kids?" queried Hon.

"Now look. On the side of each box is a sticker identifying what's inside. I've done a great job labeling all these boxes. I know what is in them. Just close that lid and stack it on the top shelf of the closet where you found it." My voice strained to maintain a calm pitch.

Undaunted, Hon continued to pillage through the cartons. "Are you keeping this paper with painted handprints all over it?"

"Oh, yes," I replied in a dreamy voice. "That's the project Sis did the second day of kindergarten. Weren't her little hands sweet? I can't throw that away!" The crinkled paper went back into the box. In fact, a lot of stuff went back into storage.

"What about these canceled checks from 1989? Don't tell me you want those for sentimental reasons," asked Hon.

"What if the FBI or the IRS investigates me?" Hon's eyes were now the size of dinner plates. "Okay, throw them out. Will you go to the prison and visit me if something happens?"

"Yes, they'll put you in the cell next to the gal who tore the warning labels off her living room sofa cushions. Man, what it takes to get anything thrown out around here." Hon exhibited strong signs of frustration and true anxiety.

"I could throw you out of here to go play golf and get a lot more accomplished." As I spoke, Hon caught a vision of hope.

"I'm not bridging this gap between trash and treasure very well," Hon said. If I promise to leave you here all alone, will you take a vow to organize this a little better?" There was a plea in his voice.

"Oh, I promise." I spent the remainder of the afternoon blissfully alone, laughing and crying over pictures and keepsakes. You know, there is something cathartic about a day like this.

All The World's A Stage

Recently, at a local football game, a friend of mine kept her right eye stuck to the viewing lens of a video camera for four solid quarters! The amazing thing about this was that she was not alone. As I looked over the crowd, there were eight more moms with eyes glued to lenses. A stranger would have thought the national networks were having a field day.

My own attempts at such recordings have met with less than favorable results, although Son has proclaimed it is wonderful that the camera adds 10 pounds to his husky appearance in a football uniform. I protest to him that I much prefer to carry my 10 pounds somewhere other than on the silver screen. Otherwise, I would have a new title. Not the Celluloid Queen, but the Cellulose Queen!

The only thing I find more interesting than the taping of each event is the cameraman who stands in the middle of a crowd of people talking to his camera. "This is Friday, Oct. 13, and Son has just gotten his shoulder pads readjusted for the third time." (All of this is intoned in a raspy pseudo-quiet voice heard on televised golf tournaments.) Yes, a person can get some strange looks while standing in the crowd giving the time and temperature like a bank sign.

It will be interesting to see what my grandchildren will do when I pull out the tapes of dear ole Sis and Son. I am sure they will have an effect similar to the one my brother wanted when he displayed the family album for my boyfriend. The friend went into hysterics and I into hysteria. I did survive, albeit I heard quips about my sailor outfit for a long time.

Whatever the outcome, this new wave reminds me of a line from Will Shakespeare's *As You Like It*: "All the world's a stage and all the men and women merely players...." What an interesting bridge giving new meaning to an old thought.

Seasonal Searches

Well, it's the first cold snap of the season and do YOU know where your woolies are? The frost rests heavily on the pumpkin and on our toes until our stored winter clothes can be located.

It's the same scenario every season, just after the temperatures drop below 70 degrees Fahrenheit. My cold-blooded, but warm-hearted, son starts playing with the thermostat and announces, "Mom, when I woke up this morning my toenails were blue and my nose red!" I truly think he should live in the tropical islands, were the lifestyle is casual and it never snows except in motion pictures. "Where did you put my electric blanket last June? You know that, since it's so cold, I'll need my long johns for yard rolling Saturday night."

"Son, you should know where to look. You put the winter clothes in the basement. Go get them. While you're down searching for underwear, bring up the afghan I always take to the football games."

Now I always hate those blank expressions I get from my children when I make what I think is a reasonable request, so I continued until I recognized a flicker of attention. "Run on down and look in the far corner. You know, the corner we're supposed to keep clear in case of a tornado or nuclear disaster."

Son disappears. I hear muffled comments and a few crashes from the bowels of my house, and in less time than it takes to load the dishwasher, he reappears with all the junk cleaned out of his room the year before, but with no winter clothes or blanket, electric or knit.

"Mom, why did you put my favorite tapes in this plastic bag? I've been looking everywhere. I even accused Sis of putting them in the garbage disposal. I can't find the winter stuff." This comes as no surprise to me. He hasn't found anything I've ever sent him in search of except food. Son will never be a famous explorer.

"Oh, I thought you didn't listen to those things anymore, so I stored them," I explained. "They might be collectors' items one of these days, so I wanted them to be in good shape." Son didn't believe that line anymore than I thought he would, but it stalled for time. "I guess you'll just have to be cold if you can't locate the winter bags. I don't have time until Saturday to look for them."

"Great, I'll freeze to death, and you'll be lost in the hundreds of boxes you've labeled 'Christmas,' which really have Halloween junk in them. I'll probably find my wool socks and sweaters packed with sparklers you bought after the Fourth of July." He stops lamenting when he notices a certain spark in my eyes. "Hey, you remember where you put 'em?"

"Yeah, there was this great box I saved from a ceiling fan I bought on sale. I'll be back in a second. Don't eat any of these cookies, they're for a meeting I've got to go to."

I returned a while later with one box of winter goods, and I knew I was safe until Sis sauntered in to request a wool scarf. I had packed the heavier things separately from the lighter ones. The other boxes and bags, crammed with gloves, tams, vests, and mothballs, would have to be located another day.

Guess that means I'll stay on this bridge until all the lost mittens can be found. Maybe it will warm up for a few days and give me a little time to continue the quest.

Gone Camping

I opened the note Son brought home from the scout meeting. It read: "This weekend is Family Camp-Out Weekend. Bring your bedrolls and canteens...it's primitive camping at Lake Lost." I slowly raised my eyes to meet Son's. He looked so eager, and I felt obligated to have our little clan represented at the campfire. I've done a lot of things to make Son and Sis know I truly love them, but this was going to be a challenging event.

Son knew that I would eventually give in and he stood stoically and waited for the go ahead for the project. "Okay, we'll be the dynamic trio on this outing." So, Son with all of his equipment, Sis with her pink bedroll, and Ma in her boots, we headed for the great outdoors of early summer. There were ten families, all with camping skills ranging from experienced and laidback to novice and nervous.

"Mom, you're a real fraidy cat. There's thirty people tromping around these woods and you're worried about wolves and cougars. If those wild animals know what's good for them, they'll high tail it back to the deep dark forest and not eat you or your cooking!" Son grinned with the security of his knowledge of the surrounding and of my fears.

"So what happens when the fire goes down and everything is quiet?" I asked. Sis, who had been forced to tag along, asked nervously as she opened her big blue eyes even wider and intently listened for a reply.

"What do you mean about the fire going out? I thought it would last 'til morning." Her whisper was a feeble attempt at bravery and got no answer, just the continuing grin.

Sis and I decided to attack the unknown problems with an organized and womanly approach. We tiptoed around the weeds, brushed and swept an area for the bed rolls and did a general inspection of the camp site. "If anything happens at least we'll know where the car is and what's in our way," I mumbled. A flashlight dangled from my neck like an albatross.

Son observed all of this and exclaimed, "You two are embarrassing me!"

"Well, you're supposed to be the Heroic One and win a badge. I'm here for the fresh air and the bonding experience of helping my first born meet one of his established goals."

"Great. You sound like a textbook." Jabbing a stick with a weenie drooping off the end in my face, he exclaimed, "Here's supper."

I whined. "I don't like hotdogs out of my own kitchen, much less handled with hands that haven't been washed since high noon yesterday."

Son had the countenance of a jailer knowing that the prisoner would eventually eat anything, and he knew I wouldn't last long. I did eat the dinner quickly. Between the bugs and the boys, no food was safe—and then, too, there's something about the outdoors that makes me hungry.

Supper wasn't all that bad, but as night fell, so did my hopes of Son wanting to go home and sleep in his own bed. The adults sat around the campfire while the mixture of siblings and scouts played radios and games in the tents. No one admitted it, but not a person there offered to go to bed first. I certainly wasn't going to bed and be the butt of any practical joke to be played. The stories and reminiscences continued well into the night and I waited until the giggles and noises ebbed into quiet.

"I think I'll go to bed. See you folks in a couple of hours."

"Be sure there's nothin' in your sleeping bag," reminded the wise leader.

I whirled around as if trying to go back in time. "What do you mean?" The panic in my voice made the pitch rise and falter like Barney Fife's.

"Oh, little critters like spiders and small snakes just love the deep soft folds of sleeping bags."

My knees began to shake and I again lost my urge to sleep. Upon entering the tent, the dank air of forest loam struck my nostrils and the lantern light gave eerie shadows to my motions. "Forget brushing teeth. Lord, my children need me. Please don't let there be anything in this bag." With the fragmented but sincere prayer, I took the cut-off handle of a rake and began to beat the bag with all the fierceness of a she-bear protecting her young. Even then, method pervaded through my madness. I'll start at the bottom and work my way inch by inch to the top. I shall not leave any section unbeaten!

"Hey, what's all the noise?" Queries from drowsy children filled the air.

"Oh, nothing, just freshening up my bag before I jump in. Boy, I'm sleepy." I pretended a yawn as I glanced to inspect the faces poking out from the covers. The children were drifting swiftly back into their slumber. Wish I could just crawl in this thing and go to sleep like everyone else. I grabbed the bottom end of the faded navy bag and bounced it up and down. If anything is in there, it will have whiplash at least.

Morning did arrive, although I never undressed or crawled into my sleeping bag. The smell of coffee and sound of conversation awoke me to the safer world of daylight. The night had seemed eternal as I crossed this bridge.

"The things we do for our children!"

"What's that you say, Mom?"

"Pass me a cup. I need caffeine and comfort right now. You know my idea of camping out is an upstairs room in a Holiday Inn."

"Okay. Oh yeah. Before you go too far, let me warn you about spiders and other leggy creatures found in the bath house." Son laughed aloud as he began the list, and I just clutched my coffee cup and started thinking of car keys and home sweet home.

Car Phone

Sis has had a life-long love affair with the telephone. I should have named her Alexandria after her hero, Alexander Graham Bell. The fact that she memorized the numbers and managed to call her grandmother long-distance at the tender age of three is testimony.

As her skills waxed strong and she grew into her adolescent years, technology blessed me with call-waiting services. If that little bit of progress had not come our way, either Sis or her mom would be in a mental institution. She continues to keep the record for having more calls on hold, and remembering more numbers than most folks I know—including very efficient secretaries!

When Sis went away to school this fall, the strangest thing happened. I had to answer my own phone again for the first time in years! And, to boot, most of the calls were for Hon and me and at normal hours of the day. Naturally, the situation automatically reverts to the familiar when Sis is back in our little nest. Example: On Saturday when most normal people watch football or do laundry, Sis is catching up with anybody else who has come home for the weekend. She doesn't even know our favorite team is two touchdowns behind. She doesn't know what the storm in the Gulf is doing. She plans to do her laundry at midnight.

I'm so accustomed to this behavior that I also revert to my predictable behavior. I put the vacuum in one of her hands and the portable phone in the other. I write notes to her telling her I'm off to the grocery store. I sometimes even make sideline remarks about the part of the conversation I hear and the interpretation of what is being said on the other end of the line. I sorta act like Florence in *The Jefferson's*. And I never even worry about where the phone is when she's home.

The ultimate progression to all of this, of course, is Sis's request for a cellular car phone. I'm all for progress, the safety factor is important, but it truly stretches my senses to think of my daughter, who needs to keep all of her attention on the highway wandering through traffic, perching a phone to her ear and reacting to the latest news just as she makes a turn. Interstate travel—she would give new definition to cruising, break speed records and wind up in Kentucky rather than Birmingham—all while chatting pleasantly on her mobile phone. I also envision the premium on her automobile insurance quadrupling.

No thanks! Experience tells me she can't do two tasks at once equally well, and if forced to choose, she would rather get a Gold Medal in Phone than a Safety Award. Sure, we'll end up getting a car phone. We can't balk on the bridge of progress too long. Sis will be pushing us too hard. But a little more time and a lot of prayer may be a prerequisite to a purchase.

Doing Time

I consider myself functionally literate, but there are occasions when I wonder. Part of this insecurity I experience is due to the biannual time change mandated by the Legislature.

I always try to remember the little phrase, "spring forward, fall back," which I have catalogued right in front of "in 1492 Columbus sailed the ocean blue," in my brain file of sometimes needed, often confused, information.

But since Columbus's century, inventors have provided thousands of ways and places to have clocks. My kitchen is one representation of this fact. The stove has three clocks, the coffeepot sports a clock, and the TV/radio blinks the hour. In order to be punctual, I keep all of these timepieces five minutes fast: I hate to be late.

Well, the Saturday afternoon before the true two a.m. turning of the clocks, I began the ritual of setting these machines.

While changing the stovetop dial, Son smirked, "Are you going to put the *real* time or are you going to put PaPa's time?"

I gave him a look of consternation and silently set the clock for the real time, although I was tempted to round the time up to the nearest half-hour as my father has always done. A flashback to my childhood swept over me. I never asked my dad for the time that I didn't get it rounded off, so the time of arrival anywhere was estimated. Dad should work for the airlines. His deep voice would be perfect for the announcement of the estimated time of arrival and the day's temperature.

Beyond the household clocks, I face the toughest challenge of all—the car clock. I get the owner's manual out and dutifully read through the instructions, but by the time I have punched all of the buttons, I have also reset all four of my radio station selections and have a curious blinking light on my dial.

When Son climbs into the front seat of an automobile, his arm automatically reaches for the radio knob and he makes his preset decision almost unconsciously. Today, however, he gives me this "what-did-you-do-to-the-radio-this-time" look as the speaker blares.

"It is nine o'clock at WUBGoo-oo-d in Chicago." I just return the stare while he sets the clock and the radio back to normal.

I breathe a sigh of relief, along with a little prayer of thanksgiving. Son is the bridge today that has helped me span necessity and invention.

Holiday Bridges

The ending of another year usually finds us dashing through bridges decorating first with pumpkins, then pilgrims, and, all too quickly, candy canes and tinsel. The events of January seem in the distant past; suddenly our gray hairs and wrinkles gaze back from the mirror. Nevertheless, 'tis the season for celebration.

November Conversations

November probably has more different celebrations within its 30 days than any other month. Now, I'm not counting National Eat Your Beets Week or anything of that sort. I'm talking real holidays, and our family conversations center around those special days. The talks begin with the ending of warm, sunny October, leaving a white blanket of toilet paper on yards and power lines and trees, thus ushering in a time of Thanksgiving and hope that we've had our turn on the All Hallows Eve.

On Tuesday morning, I announce to my children, "Today is All Saints Day at church." The puzzled looks I get back open up the round of discussion on the qualifications for sainthood.

"I don't know any saints, do I Mom?" Sis is serious, but after some explanation she decides there are a few people she knows that qualify. Son, on the other hand, can think only of a football coach or two.

The next celebration arrives in the middle of November, and, thanks to Woodrow Wilson, honors our veterans. Veterans' Day is always a good chance to wave the flag and sing lustily the patriotic songs, and to pause momentarily and think of the sacrifice handsome young men have offered to a bloody cause. We always close the program at school with the playing of taps. The eerie echoing in the gym as the lone trumpet sounds is, to me, a haunting reminder that freedom is paid for dearly. Son just hugs me when he sees the tears in my eyes after the assembly.

"Mom, what's the matter?" But he understands, and I hug him ever closer.

"Nothing's the matter. I get cold chills and deep fears when I think of having raised you only to be sacrificed on some foreign field."

It is at that instant I bond with every mother in history who has had a beloved son grow to be old enough to march away. I think I age a bit more at those moments. "If I kiss you right here in the hall, would you be too embarrassed?" Son says nothing. He has learned that, at times like this, nobody else really matters.

A couple of days later, Sis proclaims, "Thanksgiving is just a couple of weeks away. I can't wait to eat Grandmother's dressing." This next holiday of the month sneaks up on me. My body and mind keep telling me it is the last of September, but then again I think of myself as perpetually 25.

"Yeah, and there'll be lots of football games to watch and we'll be outa school." Son's blue eyes twinkle with anticipation.

"Remember, we always put up our Christmas decorations that weekend, too!" Sis squeals in childlike anticipation, thus instantly jolting me into the holiday season.

No, it's not a month away or a week away. It's here! We are in the middle of a festive bridge leading us straight into more activities. But let's do pause for a moment and appreciate the family and friends encircling us, and pray for those who protect the freedoms we celebrate.

Veterans' Day

As we approach another November 11th to give pause and tribute to all the people who have served our country, I can't help but think of my maternal grandfather. Grandfather Wright, like many red-blooded family men all over the country, joined the navy after the bombing of Pearl Harbor and shipped out of San Francisco on the USS *South Dakota* and straight into the battle zones of the Pacific theater.

He left a loving wife and three children—an average life filled with comfortable and simple routine—for the harrowing nightmare of a world war. My quiet, soft-spoken grandfather loaded the guns of a battleship, and dreamed of his wife Audrey.

He was one of the lucky ones—he only broke a foot during his tour of duty. And as the war came to its cataclysmic end on September 2, 1945, his ship was in Tokyo Harbor alongside the USS *Missouri* as Generals MacArthur and Umezu signed the peace treaty to finally end the carnage. "We climbed everything on the ship in order to get a better view. We were a part of history. I'll never forget." And, indeed, he didn't.

One of my childhood memories is Grandfather's bedroom in the white house out in the rural farmland of north Alabama. The western windows of the small room looked out on a big, peaceful oak tree with a tire swing and sheltering a picnic table. Inside, on the western wall, hung a picture of his battleship. It was strange and out of place, this framed image of a massive machine of war on old-fashioned flowered wallpaper. Even then, as a small child, the incongruity of this image struck me.

Grandfather spoke about the black and white photograph only when asked, and then in an almost church-like reverence. He never told us the real stories. I'm sure they were too hurtful and horrible, and, as children, we were to be spared the brutal details of buddies lost, of oblations made.

I did not comprehend the full implications of war and personal tragedies until my junior year in high school, when Vietnam claimed the fun-loving youths of my world. And then, years later, when the Gulf War loomed heavy and my son was old enough to go to war, the picture came back to my mind's eye. Clear and sharp like the lines of the ship in my grandfather's photograph of cold gray metal, it stood for the tenets of American life: family, safety, peace. It represented long, lonely months away from homeplace under the shade of the oaks.

I wish my grandfather were still here to celebrate peace and to tell his story to his great-grandchildren, to show them the photograph, but he's not. Yet, as each successive generation crosses its own bridge of patriotic sacrifice, a nation discovers that we still remember, still hold to the ideals of liberty, still ask the unassuming men to put down the tools of peace, take up the death tools, and still carry our photographs to the wall and in our hearts.

As a nation we say *thanks* and we *remember* on each 11th hour of the 11th day of the 11th month.

Veterans' Day Salute

I had a chance to visit Washington, D.C., this past summer. The July sun beat down mercilessly on my shoulders as I strolled past the Reflecting Pool and the Lincoln Memorial. Of course, the Smithsonian and National Gallery were on my list of things to see and do in the Capitol, but my mission on this particular day was to view the Wall.

The last time I walked this path 15 years ago, the memorial to the Vietnam soldiers did not exist, nor did the Korean Memorial, nor the Nurses' Memorial. Therefore, being a child of the '60's, I felt welling up inside me the need to locate, to see, and touch the name of my high school friend. For years, he appeared on the list of MIAs, but the reality of time moved his name to the chronological list of casualties.

Walter was an only son and the baby brother of three very protective older sisters. He sat quietly in classes and church, planning his future and setting simple goals, but the draft and Asia abruptly changed all of that. He didn't fit on a battlefield, and the paradox of this soft-spoken child of peace being thrust into the violence and turmoil of war confuses me even now.

In the welcomed shade of an oak tree, I respectfully turned the pages of the massive registry and jotted down a section and line, then walked toward the famous black scar in the Capitol's ground. Like so many of the millions of visitors who have stood before this simple listing of the dead, my throat tightened with emotion as my eyes scanned the engraved names. It read like a random collection from the nations of the world: Polasky, Lancaster, Trudeau, Romanoff—like the melting pot America is.

Tears dripped from under my sunglasses, and the slick marble cooled my fingertips, but not my thoughts as I rubbed the crayon over the slip of paper the guard had given me. Walter's name appeared as if by magic. I had finally crossed a bridge I had avoided for 30 years. There has never been a body to bury in the plot next to his father, and, although he once was lost, I had found Walter at peace with his buddies surrounding him. I walked away in silence, sharply aware that his name appeared in one of the first of a long stretch of panels.

Freedom comes to each generation at a dear price. From the soldiers in Washington's army, who struggled with the elements and championed freedom, to the soldiers of the Gulf War, it is fitting we should stop and respectfully salute them all on this Veterans' Day.

Simple Thanks

My folks raised me to be thankful and to appreciate the simple things of everyday life and I have tried to pass these values on to my children.

While blow-drying her hair one Tuesday morning, Sis asked, "What are you most thankful for, Mom?"

At the moment, it was the fact we were ten minutes ahead of schedule but, "Oh, lots of things," began my listing. "I'm very thankful I can get into my winter clothes, that my shoe size is now smaller than yours, that my little red car has made it another year without a major blowup, and that my legs aren't as hairy as Son's."

Sis truly thought this approach to thankfulness a bit unusual, but only fluffed and sprayed her bangs.

I rambled on, naming things every true-hearted American mother would mention: Ziplock bags, service station attendants who still wash windshields, earphones, mothballs, and insect repellents.

"Mom, come down to earth."

"Oh, I'm thankful for bigger things, too!" I quipped. For example: I don't live in Bosnia, and I don't have to worry about security guards for all my valuables. I'm thankful we still have a roof even after two storms this year. I'm thankful Hon has a remote control which emits a signal to help him find it in the crevices of the couch. I'm thankful for computers when they actually do what they are supposed to do." Sensing the serious mood of the moment, I pecked her freckled cheek. "I'm thankful for how good you and Son both are and how interesting you make every day. I get to see the world through another set of eyes and that keeps me thinking."

I could tell that was a revelation, a bridge on which to pause and ponder. She was warmed by what I had said, and so was I. I vowed to share such insights more often.

Thanks A Lot!

I was driving down the road listening to the radio a day or two ago when a song by a well-known country band began to play. The theme of the song was "Thank You, the Working Man." As I drove, I tapped my finger to the snappy beat, and I enjoyed the message as well. There are a lot of everyday people in my life who need thanking, so this one's for you.

Thank you, checkout people. Your smile and greeting when I've had a long day and had to buy groceries or glue before cooking supper, brightens my moment. It reminds me that your shifts are also long, but the smile is there.

Thank you, secretaries. You make the calls and do the millions of tasks that make an office run smoothly, and with patience you take the calls of all those irate, confused customers.

Thank you, repair people. You fix my broken stuff and don't laugh when I can't make the same sound as my car; and you know that although I don't cook often, my stove working properly is a psychological thing. And I understand that plumbing is more than cutting the water off and just replacing a part, and you know that plumbing is essential.

Thank you, farmers. You keep alive the people with no green thumb, and those without the inclination to have one. But you also keep alive the belief in good, hardworking, simple people who care about their neighbors and love God and country deeply.

And that, in turn, leads me to thank all the cooks and waitresses who strive to please more picky people than I have ever had to please at my table. It's hot in the kitchen in July, and lonely during the holidays. Thanks for serving another cup of coffee while friends hash out the events of their lives, and for twirling the ice cream a little more for a child.

Thank you, ministers and nurses. You ease the crises of our lives and give us hugs and prayers when words are not enough. Those times are never forgotten.

Thank you, policeman, firefighter, teacher, coach, child-care worker. The thousands of deeds you do that will never be lauded are important to every child you pat with encouragement and every family you help.

To the cosmetologist who is the common person's psychiatrist, to the bank teller, the person at the window at the fast-food place, to everyone who serves people with a smile: *Thank you* for making the bridges of life more comfortable and more pleasant to cross.

Stuffed Turkey

Parents don't ever grant children credit for being able to chew gum and walk at the same time. The concept stems from all the times in our growing-up lives we truly *couldn't* simultaneously chew gum and walk. We proved it to them time and again. But, alas, there did come a day in my adulthood when I had a chance to prove myself worthy of my folks' respect.

It was a "gotcha" kinda day. Thanksgiving, 1975. "Here I am in middle America, grown and properly married with children, holding down a steady job, and my Dad doesn't want to come to my house for Thanksgiving! He thinks I can't cook a real meal!" I stirred another lump of sugar into my coffee, and my best friend smiled.

"Honey, you may see the polar ice caps thaw before you get verbal credit for being able to do normal kinds of things, much less do a respectable job on such an important family occasion." Martha always spoke truisms with a voice so full of authority God took notes.

"Yeah, I just can't shake the image or smell of my burning two entire sheets of peanut butter cookies or melting an aluminum TV dinner. And the time I left out the sugar in an apple pie, everybody at the table gagged and vowed revenge. There's plenty of proof, I'm afraid. He might be right." I finished my cup of coffee and poured another. This conversation had the potential to turn into a full pot session, and I slid deep into my chair to listen to my enlightened friend.

"Well, this is your chance to prove them wrong. I've got the perfect recipe for roasting a turkey until it's golden brown." She explained every detail and I took copious notes, but just in case there might be a problem,

I wrote her phone number in bold strokes at the top of the page. Determination set in, but with a Plan A and Plan B. I would cook this turkey by the prescribed rules, but if it didn't turn out according to the directions, then Plan B would be in place—calling the local deli, which advertised complete meals for the holiday at a reasonable price.

I shopped and cleaned and decorated for the big day. Martha chuckled to herself every time we chatted. A couple of days before Thanksgiving we sat across from each other, tired from all the tasks.

"I hope I've got everything." I shoved her my list of ingredients and supplies. I felt it was a sign from heaven when she nodded approval. "But I think I'll cook this bird the day before so, if I need to proceed to Plan B, I'll have time."

"That's a coward's way out, but maybe you're a smart coward! Remember to give that bird several days to thaw out or you'll be on the phone to the deli."

I struggled and stuffed, basted and basked. My turkey sat in the platter just like the golden one in Rockwell's famous *Saturday Evening Post* cover! My folks were to arrive at 11:00 and I was ready. I dialed Martha to preen and gloat.

"Would you like to have some fun?" Her voice held a tantalizing tone of mischief. "I have a supermarket replica of a twenty-pound Butterball my dad used for display. It looks exactly like the ones in the freezer case." I listened to her plan and grinned.

My folks arrived with the usual flurry of greetings, hugs, and inspection, until Dad glanced at the kitchen counter. There sat a frosty turkey still sheathed in plastic and netting.

"I thought I'd wait until you got here to cook the turkey," I said in as blasé, a voice as I could muster. The expression on Dad's face would surely have won me a TV prize if I had captured it on film, but, alas, the moment passed quickly. "I haven't read the directions yet...."

"Don't you know that it takes hours to...."

I broke into hysterical laughter and picked up the plastic bird, gave it a twirl, then produced my picture-perfect turkey, placed it in the middle of my festive table, and winked, "Gotcha! Happy Thanksgiving."

Open Letters

As my family gathers around the table this Thanksgiving Day, I have so many things for which I need to say, "Thanks." So, here is an open letter to God on this important day.

Dear God,

The first thing I want to give thanks for is living in a country at peace. There have been Thanksgiving dinners when sons have be in combat half a world away and our thoughts were occupied with their safety. This November, our troops are camped around family fires and not the bonfires of war. Thanks.

Like the old hymn, "For the Beauty of the Earth," I want to express to you my appreciation for the place I live. The mountains are ruggedly beautiful, and fields in their different phases are wondrous and exciting to watch. From delicate spring, to August summer, from lusty fall, to quiet winter, there is craftsmanship in the seasons you create.

And, dear Lord, I must say that the sunsets you have painted for me to see from seacoast to front yard have been outstanding. As I gaze upon the colors and composition of your artistry, I stand in awe. Thanks.

The friends you have scattered into my pathway are as different and unexpected sometimes as the snowflakes of January. Thanks for the listeners, the helpers, the entertainers, and the constant. Without them, I wouldn't be able to keep my refrigerator or my car fixed, would not understand myself or my teenagers, nor could I laugh over a cup of coffee at the situations we get stuck in sometimes. They are all invaluable. Thanks.

And thanks for my family. They have watched me change and grow with patience and love. My life would be dull and cold without the blanket of aunts, uncles, grandparents, and children. In your supreme wisdom, you have also given me the extended family of people who sometimes know me better than I know myself, and love me anyway. Thanks.

As I close this letter to you this day, I must thank you for all the bridges. Some I have dashed across, others I have stumbled through, while there has been one or two this year that you have had to lift me up and carry me across. Thanks.

Christmas Shopping

As traditional as Thanksgiving leftovers is the American ritual of "the Friday after" shopping trip. After the feast comes the fiasco and the fury of hoards of bargain hunters.

Knowing deep down in my heart that shopping malls the day after Thanksgiving are battle zones with women armed with plastic and carts rather than bazookas, I naively fantasized that this year would be different. Hey, wasn't this supposed to be the season for peace on earth? Flipping through all the newspaper ads, I made my list and checked it twice. And Thursday night, armed with my trusty list, I announced over a turkey sandwich, "I think I can finish my Christmas shopping in one day. The sales start at six a.m. and there are extra specials for the early birds."

Hon's eyebrows almost met his hairline. "Sweetheart, I have prayed for miracles, but it would be an event bigger than Moses parting the Red Sea if that did indeed happen." Unbelievingly, he chomped on stuffed celery sticks and searched for the remote. "I think there's a golf tournament from Hawaii on and at least one football game. You don't want me to go with you, do you?" A glimpse of a mall full of eager consumers, along with the two of us attempting to get something done, brought a look of panic on both our faces.

In a mock-pacifying tone I consoled, "No thanks, Sis is going with me. There's plenty of dressing and mashed potatoes in the kitchen for lunch tomorrow. We'll be home no later than Christmas Eve." Hon nodded absently as he flipped the channels.

Friday morning broke with a picturesque sunrise and child-like hope. At 5:30 the parking lot of the mall teemed with people and cars. With the aid of binoculars, I could almost see the entrance from our parking space. "Guess they don't call these shoes 'cross-trainers' for nothing," I said. "We can get our two-mile walk done and arrive at the first sale at the same time." Sis didn't appreciate the humor.

Inside, sale signs draped every store entrance. I pulled out my list and darted for the first table of items. "I'm glad hunting socks have been marked down 50 percent. Son needs a size...."

About that time a female the height and weight of an NFL tackle snatched the pair right out of my hands. I gulped and waited for the blow, but instead she vanished into the swarm of arms surrounding the counter. "Maybe I'll go to the next store and shop for the Legos."

"I'll get us a buggy for protection." Sis pushed forward like a real trouper, but even this simple task was fraught with problems. "Either the aisles have shrunk, or the carts are bigger," she whined. The kid was telling the truth. The California freeways at rush hour could not be more congested, nor the drivers more rude. Yes, indeed, holiday spirits were high; red faces glowed with impatience at every turn and boxes of toys teetered dangerously over the entire scene. A frazzled salesclerk brushed a sprig of garland back from her face and offered assistance.

"Please help me find the Power Ranger doll with...."

The gal cut me short. "Sold out of those three days ago, and, *no*, we will not be restocking before February." She turned on her heels satisfied that she had done her duty.

I half-heartedly picked up a clone of the doll and headed for the checkout. Doom and gloom fell heavily on my holiday cheer. The line looked like the entire population of the state stood in a single queue.

"I'm not crossing this bridge today," I said as I plopped the toy back into its slot on the shelf, thus causing an avalanche of accessories onto my head! Sis and I gazed at each other, then broke into hysterical laughter.

"Remember, your bridge to the parking lot is two miles long, but at least we don't have any heavy packages to carry," I reminded.

But we still managed to hum the "Hallelujah Chorus" as we swung open the exit doors and entered the brilliant sunshine.

On, Dasher!

As though some mischievous little elf has sneaked into town and strung up all the lights and glitter, the race toward Christmas season has begun. With the motion lights twinkling, the family instantly dashes into planning and holiday activity with the last of the Thanksgiving turkey.

"Hey, when does the tree go up?" Sis quizzed as I drove her to school. "I think we ought to decorate it with those pretty pink lace bows with strings of pearls."

"Oh, yes. Those sweet little dolls with ribbons and lace are so cute," I agreed.

The idealistic gleam in her blue eyes was extinguished quickly by Son's reply as we rounded the corner. "You two twinkies put pink and lace on our tree and the protest will be loud enough to be heard in Washington state. Who ever heard of pink on a tree! That's not even a Christmas color." He began to sulk as the notion threatened to become reality. I pondered these things in my heart and decided not to show him the latest ladies' journal with all those gorgeous Victorian trees.

We dash to the tree farm, then make the hundreds of trips to the basement for decorations, swirl the branches with lights, hang the traditional and sentimental ornaments, and stand back to see that is good. Son is at peace and Sis is pleased with the esthetics of our labors, but not a moment is to be spared.

"Okay, I didn't volunteer you for a dozen cookies this year. I don't have time to make them, and the ones you bought for the last party were fed to the birds." By now, Sis begins to develop the countenance of a

Congressman discussing the practical facts of an unpleasant task. "But, I do have three places to be Tuesday afternoon." On, Dasher!

With a pace only a mother can keep, the season rushes on with a spectacular fury. Parties, practices, plays come and go with the weeks. "You know, Santa Claus is watching you. Clean up your spot in the den. Meet me at the hamburger joint one more time and I promise I'll cook some *real* food tomorrow. Run pick up more wrapping paper so you can take these gifts to the collection at the church." Both kids stare in disbelief.

"Mom, I know you don't want a stroke, so would you please give us a break? And for goodness sake, don't play that Andy Williams album again unless you use the earphones." Son has determination in his voice. "You've been like that whatchamacallit endangered darting fish. You don't want to become endangered, do you?"

"Okay, sit down and I'll fix us a cup of hot chocolate and some cinnamon toast. Don't you like Andy Williams' Christmas album? I think..."

His expression freezes my words. Think I've dashed enough through this bridge. I'll slow down and sniff the cocoa and spice of life and the season.

Oh, Christmas Tree!

I love Christmas—the maddening crowds, the billions of calories, tinsel, glitter, and the traditions, one of which is the selecting and placing of the family Christmas tree.

The last few years, Sis and I have cut our traditional tree at a local farm. There pervades a pioneer spirit that stirs us as we tramp over what seems to be hundreds of acres before earmarking our choice. It takes the better part of the morning to check for holes and height, but after the decision is made, the felling begins.

Sis gnaws at the trunk with a bow saw that must have been used to build eighteenth century log cabins, and even after struggling at cutting, the trunk seems petrified and doesn't offer to lean. So, I give it a whack or two. By this time, all the winter clothes, worn with the thought of going out in cold weather to cut trees, has had to be shed. Only in storybooks and beer commercials are Christmas trees cut in pristine snow and placed on a sleigh with bells and beautiful horses. Not in Alabama.

Working up a sweat and an appetite in the humid morning air and accomplishing absolutely nothing with our efforts, I place Sis squarely in front of the evergreen, just like I was staking a claim for gold, and announce that I'm going for help. Tree farmers are nice to help stranded pioneers, and with two or three powerful drags across the trunk, the tree collapses.

After the shaking and loading, Sis and I sing right along with the Robert Shaw Chorale as we head home knowing our biggest challenge is yet to be conquered.

Hon and sidekick Son are at home watching some football team play for national recognition. They give us an insulting glare when we pronounce to duo that *our* tree needs to be placed in the stand and brought inside.

"You've really picked a winner this time, Mom. Get me a blue ribbon," Son caustically replies. I soon realize I have again chosen a tree much too tall for our room, that it has no "good side," and that the trunk is crooked. It never ceases to amaze me that the tree that appears perfect in the forest is consumed with flaws indoors.

Perry Como and Andy Williams are now strongly competing for air waves with Brian Gumble and the Golden Force of some state university and the wailing of Son over the interruption of his sports ritual.

"If you stick the tree in that corner, we won't be able to see "Wheel of Fortune!" until January!" moans Hon.

"Yeah, I'll have to read the bowl results in the paper 'cause, I'll never be able to see the games," says Son.

I give both offspring and my spouse my Medusa look, and stubborn silence pervades as the tree is relegated to the far corner, leaving behind a trail of needles from the kitchen to the living room.

I sit down with a mug of chocolate and hum along with Mitch Miller and the gang, "Oh, Christmas tree, oh, Christmas tree...." My thoughts drift past the words to the symbols of the evergreen used for centuries to represent eternal life, and our tree is a living bridge to now be adorned with symbols and celebrations of the past and present.

Christmas Lights

I know you've seen the hardware store commercial with the couple trying to untangle a set of Christmas lights. The producer must have over-heard our discussion Sunday night.

"Okay, the tree is in the stand and now we're ready for the lights," Hon said as he brushed his mustache and wiped his brow. Usually, at eight o'clock at night, the last thing on his mind is Christmas lights, but he has ESP when it comes to realizing that he won't get any rest until I'm content with my new Christmas tree glowing in its corner.

I pulled three boxes labeled "tree lights" down from the attic with self-congratulation for having been able to find them in record time. "Here! All the strands, they've been individually wrapped. This should be an easy task." The statement could not have been further from the truth. Yes, each strand of 150 white lights had been separately bagged, but that didn't pre-vent the mess which began to unfold.

"Mom, test all these little rascals before we string them on the tree. Remember, last year we had a thousand lights, but only 750 of them actu-ally burned all season," says Son.

It was true. Each group plugged, each bulb hand tested, and still we had half a set in the middle of the fir tree burn out before December 12.

Hon looked worried. The clock ticked loudly and his eyelids drooped. "It's a scheme by the Christmas lights people to make sure folks have to buy several new sets every year. The problem is we can't remember which sets are new and which ones are just waiting to burn out after we put them up."

Son woke up from his football game stupor to interject, "Why don't we just trash the lights every year and buy new ones. They always have them on sale. You wouldn't have to store them, or spend six hours untangling them and tangling up your nerves."

All of us glared and Son returned to the tube. We launched the trial run on the floor, and things seemed pretty good. Two sets for the garbage, one set to use outside, and six sets for the tree.

Bravely, Sis suggested we get started. "We've got everything out, so let's string up the lights before we go to bed. The tree's smaller than the one last year, so we'll have enough sets."

"You're so cheerful you sound like Tiny Tim," Son said, his voice sounding more like Scrooge.

"Okay, let's do it." Hon plunged into the next phase of the project with the all energy he could muster. "Round and round, in and out—things are looking good...." Crunch! "There goes one more set!" Backing up to admire his work, Hon had stepped on an awaiting strand. Son burst into laughter, Sis's eyes widened, and I grabbed the vacuum.

For all his pseudo-cynicism, Son rose to the occasion. "I'll go to the all-night grocery and pick up another bunch. Need anything else while I'm there? Milk, bread, nerve pills?"

"No, but this bridge is too familiar."

"That's because it happens the same way every year, and it will go on happening until we stop having Christmas trees with lights," said Son. He swooped up his keys and then turned back to a weary trio slumped on the couch. Hon's snores already echoed through the room. Grinning like the Grinch, Son exclaimed 'ere he drove out of sight, "Merry Christmas to all, and to all a good night."

No-Bake Christmas

I cook good enough to stave off hunger, and acknowledge fact that I am no contestant for Julia Child's School of Culinary Arts. Whatever I manage to put on the table, even if I follow the magazine recipe, has never even resembled the full-page colored picture.

Starting in October, the ladies' magazines launch their spreads of Christmas cooking and decorations. I browse with interest and respect through the dazzling displays, which must have calories even in the air the pages fan. As I flip the pages, I could hang the person responsible for the notion that a working mother with two teenagers should have to cook her way from Halloween to New Year's.

Sis bounced in from school a few afternoons ago announcing as she searched the refrigerator shelves, "Mom, I've got to have two dozen home-baked cookies for our club's Christmas meeting in the morning." Slamming the door shut, she retreated to her room empty-handed.

In all honesty, I must explain that news like this always hits me like the aftershocks of a California earthquake. Recovering from the reality that I must cook immediately, I pulled Sis from her afternoon game show and phone call decreeing that, if she had to have my original recipe by 8 a.m., we would make them before 8 a.m.

Pulling out an old cookie recipe didn't take much effort, but the events which transpired did. We proceeded to flour and cut and cook. We cut stars, camels, Santas, and angels, and shoved them in the oven to bake. By the time the batches were hatched, the kitchen looked as if a white Christmas might be possible.

Sniffing the air and smelling food, Son appeared at the sink while the sheets of cookies cooled. "What's that supposed to be?" he inquired as he poked the first of two handfuls of unidentified baked objects into his mouth.

"Never mind. What do they taste like?"

"Like thick biscuits!"

Sis and I just gazed at each other. We were covered with flour and dough, tired, and filled with dismay.

"Get your coat. The deli is still open. We'll put two dozen cookies in the pretty angel tin. But be warned, I'll use you for reindeer bait if you breathe a word about purchasing our homemade cookies from the all-night supermarket."

We agreed and went over a river and through a bridge to buy our Christmas goodies.

All Wrapped Up

There is little doubt in my mind that, in some remote corner of the North Pole, the elf who manufactures Christmas wrapping paper has never seen the manner in which some of my presents have been disguised. He must also get a percentage of the profit on the rolls and rolls of paper and the miles and miles of tape I've bought over the last decade and be paid double for the rolls bought early, stored, then lost. It is one of my recurrent problems.

Because I took lessons from the older generation of Christmas shoppers in my family, I have purchased paper for the holiday season as early as July. I admit it seems a little early, but when the trees are decorated and displayed and the lights blink, what can I do to resist? In my mind, I rationalize the purchase by convincing myself that I have saved a great deal of money and time. So when I do start to buy the gifts on my list, I have something to wrap them in immediately.

But nothing in my life works according to plans, and by December I have tucked the bundles of designed paper in some unremembered place. It must be noted that I usually do find all five or six boxes of gift wrap after I buy new paper at regular price (shudder, shudder) and have begun placing packages under the tree.

Regarding those lovely decorative boxes needing no wrapping paper, I did use them one year. Unfortunately, the sides of the boxes kept collapsing, and the shirts kept falling out. The boxes looked as if they had been hit by a Big Pig transfer truck.

Then, there is the likelihood that there is not enough paper of the same pattern to wrap an odd-sized or a big box, (meaning I have to piece my paper much like my neighbor pieces her quilts, or use more paper than is really needed, leaving corners to tape that look like the work of my two-year-old nephew). Gifts such as umbrellas, vases, and tennis gear provide many creative opportunities to the poor, tired mother trying to make merry the lives of her children and friends.

Then, there was the year I decided I would wrap all my presents in the same paper, just like in the ladies' magazines. That worked pretty well until I ran out of paper. I had bought the stuff on sale the day after Christmas 1986, and there was no new paper out to match. That episode ended my monochromatic era.

But perhaps the most enduring and aggravating problem of wrapping is keeping up with the tape, scissors, and name tags until all packages are secured and delivered. Tape dispensers should stick to the drawers into which placed or give off alarm signals if moved by unauthorized personnel. I never get prepared to start the task of wrapping without a word of prayer: "Please, help me find my tape and scissors within the hour." I tried everything, from putting strings on each and tying them to the counter, to buying a set for each room. Nothing has helped so far.

Inevitably, then, on every list I make at Christmas, I put paper, tape, scissors, and name tags. Maybe the person who thinks up all these little gimmicks for the home shopping audience will invent a gadget and help me to bridge the hopelessness of this problem to the brighter tomorrow I always search for with the holidays.

First One Up

There's one in every family. You know, the kid who gets up in the middle of the night to see what Santa Claus has delivered. My middle brother wins the prize in our clan.

For all our childhood years, each Christmas Eve, at 6 p.m. he would begin to hustle our youngest brother and me. "You gotta go to bed. Santa Claus will pass us by 'cause we won't be asleep." To a set of pre-computer kids under ten years old this made perfect sense, especially when supported by the concurrent nods of our parents. I'm sure the earlier we proceeded to bed, for them, the better.

Much to my folks' chagrin, this concept of early to bed went hand in hand with the rest of the familiar phrase: early to rise. In the middle of the night while three of us still counted sugar plums and Dad snored, number two child's eyes would open as if possessed by a spell. Zombie-like, he would creep into the living room and locate all the goodies awaiting discovery. After memorizing each display, testing each toy, and shaking each wrapped box, he would then proceed to his dark room and the bottom bunk bed and his slumbering brother.

"Ps-ss-t, you got a Texaco service station with a ramp and four cars. It's neat. I'll swap my Mickey Mantle baseball game for it." He would poke and shake and squeal. Of course, it didn't take long for the little fellow to be on the cold floor and dashing like Santa's reindeer to find the toys beneath the tree. And, once he was occupied, it was my turn.

Striding confidently to my bedside, child number two would energetically proclaim the treasures left for me. "The doll Santa left for you has eyes that close. Hey, it walks and wets, too. I gave her a full bottle of water just to check her out. Gonna use a lot of diapers!"

"What about my new diary? Did he leave a blue one with a key like I asked for in my letter?" I query with only one eye open, and with all my other senses shut down.

Tugging at the quilt, he said, "Sure did. And there's all kinds of stocking stuff. Get up and come see."

Cradling a Betsy Wetsy doll and hiding the diary in record time came as second nature to a sister with *two* male siblings. About that time, Mom and Dad would stagger wearily into the room, nodding answers to questions. As I recall, they were pretty non-verbal.

"Man, I'm tired. Think I'll go back to bed for awhile," yawns the instigator.

"Me, too!" The younger partner pronounces as he grabs a truck to take with him to assure that it has not been a dream.

"Good! Let's all get a couple of hours more sleep and then I'll cook a big breakfast," suggests Mom, adding the cheerily appropriate phrase borrowed from Dickens' *A Christmas Carol*, "God Bless Us Every One." It must be a Mom thing to always have great timing and wonderful ideas. Therefore, with that notion giving us all that warm fuzzy feeling of having a dream come true, the entire brood would be exonerated and head back to bed with a kiss and a pat on each tousled head.

And we'd hear my brother exclaim as he dozed off to sleep. "Hey, Merry Christmas, everybody!"

A Good Christmas Laugh

Most of the time when folks reach back to their remembrances of Christmas, they return to poignant, sad, or faintly melancholy cameos. We solemnly recall family and friends, God and His gift, but I have a favorite Christmas memory that brings tears of laughter.

It was a Christmas from my middle childhood, and my two younger brothers and I had asked for matching Roy Rogers and Dale Evans cowboy suits. Western wear was all the rage. And since the Santa Claus of my youth worked miracles, it's a wonder we didn't each order a palomino horse to go along with the outfits. We didn't get gifts during the year, but we always got what we asked for, and more, under the tree on Christmas morning.

On that Christmas Eve night, Santa deposited our gifts in designated corners of the living room, ate the chocolate chip cookies, drank the milk, and left the empty saucer and glass in a very obvious place on the coffee table. This particular year, a handwritten note rested on the wrinkled napkin, but we didn't bother to read the message. There were surprises to be checked out and stuff to be scattered all over the house.

And, yes, the cowboy ensembles were there that year—chocolate brown with white leather fringe—with gloves imprinted with cowboys and horses! As I stood in front of the mirror, I made the best-dressed Dale in Alabama. But there was one big problem. In place of a beautiful Stetson, I had a net-covered, green army helmet! Mom gently suggested I read aloud the letter from Santa to my brothers, who by this time were also decked out in helmets.

The note apologized for Santa running completely out of cowboy hats. He hoped these modern, metallic replacements would do.

Being a child of nine or so, I did not really question the omnipotent power of the Claus or my folks, who were now busy arranging their trio of strangely dressed dudes for the traditional photo shoot. My brothers never seemed to notice the incongruity. We posed by the holly bushes in the front yard, and I am sure the people who drove by wondered at the sight. And what a sight. Three grinning stairstep children dressed in fringed holsters, cap pistols and ammunition, topped with helmets and looking as if we were part of the 2nd Infantry!

Even now while at the kitchen table when my brothers and I reminisce, we laugh and relish the memory of that Christmas after having faced dilemmas of equal magnitude with our own children. We detect the creative interpretation Santa had to the problem, and, from experience, know the present can certainly learn from the past. I suspect the lesson is the bridge Mom and Dad constructed with understanding and good humor.

Ready And Set

I have come to the conclusion that the reason for staying up until the stroke of midnight on December 31st is to officially mark the marathon of bowl games played on New Year's Day. There is not another day on the calendar to rival the mania displayed by masses of people over teams, scores, and ratings.

I look forward to watching the Rose Bowl Parade. The beautiful floats made from zillions of flower petals are truly an amazing thing to behold. Last year, as I sat discussing the brilliant colors with Sis, a sweat-shirted thief snatched the remote control and flipped to a game in progress. To add confusion to mayhem, I observed a procession of what must have been every television set in the neighborhood lining up in my living room.

"Hey, what's going on here? Does this look like Circuit City to you?" Even as I spoke, a parade of teenage male football fans, each bearing his own personal remote control, plopped in front of a screen. "You guys look as if you're digging in for the duration." No truer words have ever been uttered, for, as I recall, no one moved for the next 18 hours except to jump up in disgust at a play or to rejoice over a victory.

"Mom do you think you could pop us some popcorn and bring us a liter of Coke?" The request was delivered without Son turning his head or releasing the control.

"Sure, and I'll bring in a bowl of lizard's legs and frog guts, too."

"Thanks, Mom. You're great."

Among the host of football fiends punching and yelling as teams fended and fell was a shy, mannerly fellow who gave me such a questioning look I felt the need to continue the ruse. "Can I get anything special for you? I have a kitchen full of goodies." The child, horrified at the request, shook his head violently. He seemed to lose his concentration after that, for, as I brought in the bowls of popcorn, he jumped up with an excuse of being late to his grandmother's hundredth birthday party and slammed the door behind him.

The others just plowed into the refreshments without a glance. I could have put bugs, rocks, liver—anything I chose—into the mixture, for all were still affixed to the games in front of them.

By 8 p.m. the shoulders of the crowd began to droop and football fatigue set in, and by halftime of the Orange Bowl (which I always make it a point to watch), three of the boys were comatose. At precisely the last second of the last game, all seven collapsed as if the starch had suddenly gone out of their spines.

"Why don't I just cover you boys with blankets and turn off all the TV sets?"

A faint reply came from the direction of the couch. "No, they'll give highlights of all the games in just a minute."

Nothing but astonishment filled my face. Why would any human soul put himself on such a bridge of endurance and frustration for hours and then ask for more? I didn't get an answer, for the youngster just turned over on the rug with his eyes fixed and hand frozen. I tried to comfort him with a little motherly patting of the shoulder as I turned off all the sets.

Someone muttered as the silence fell, "What a way to start a new year!"